Herman Melville's
BILLY BUDD,
BENITO CERENO, &
BARTLEBY THE SCRIVENER

NOTES

Edited and with an Introduction by
HAROLD BLOOM

Printed and bound in the United States of America.

First Printing
1 3 5 7 9 8 6 4 2

ISBN: 0-7910-4083-6

Chelsea House Publishers
1974 Sproul Road, Suite 400
P.O. Box 914
Broomall, PA 19008-0914

Contents

User's Guide

This volume is designed to present biographical, critical, and bibliographical information on Herman Melville and *Billy Budd,* "Benito Cereno," and "Bartleby the Scrivener." Following Harold Bloom's introduction, there appears a detailed biography of the author, discussing the major events in his life and his important literary works. Then follows a thematic and structural analysis of the works, in which significant themes, patterns, and motifs are traced. An annotated list of characters supplies brief information on the chief characters in the work. A selection of critical extracts, derived from previously published material by leading critics, then follows. The extracts consist of such things as statements by the author on his works, early reviews of the works, and later evaluations down to the present day. The items are arranged chronologically by date of first publication. A bibliography of Melville's writings (including a complete listing of all books he wrote, cowrote, edited, and translated, and selected posthumous publications), a list of additional books and articles on him and on *Billy Budd,* "Benito Cereno," and "Bartleby the Scrivener," and an index of themes and ideas conclude the volume.

Harold Bloom is Sterling Professor of the Humanities at Yale University and Henry W. and Albert A. Berg Professor of English at the New York University Graduate School. He is the author of twenty books and the editor of more than thirty anthologies of literature and literary criticism.

Professor Bloom's works include *Shelley's Mythmaking* (1959), *The Visionary Company* (1961), *Blake's Apocalypse* (1963), *Yeats* (1970), *A Map of Misreading* (1975), *Kabbalah and Criticism* (1975), and *Agon: Towards a Theory of Revisionism* (1982). *The Anxiety of Influence* (1973) sets forth Professor Bloom's provocative theory of the literary relationships between the great writers and their predecessors. His most recent books are *The American Religion* (1992) and *The Western Canon* (1994).

Professor Bloom earned his Ph.D. from Yale University in 1955 and has served on the Yale faculty since then. He is a 1985 MacArthur Foundation Award recipient and served as the Charles Eliot Norton Professor of Poetry at Harvard University in 1987–88. He is currently the editor of the Chelsea House series Major Literary Characters and Modern Critical Views, and other Chelsea House series in literary criticism.

Introduction

HAROLD BLOOM

Herman Melville's *The Piazza Tales* (1856) is the best of his fiction after *Moby-Dick* (1851). Modern critical opinion adds the short novel, *Billy Budd,* first published in 1924, a third of a century after Melville's death. By general consent, the two most powerful of *The Piazza Tales* are "Benito Cereno" and "Bartleby the Scrivener," though I myself judge "The Encantadas" and "The Bell-Tower" to be of almost equal eminence.

As a parable of Melville's own self-alienation, *Billy Budd* has extraordinary poignance, though the writer seems immensely distanced from the tale he tells. If *Moby-Dick* on so many levels is a Gnostic dispute with the God of the Bible, particularly the God of Job and of Jonah, *Billy Budd* instead stations itself beyond any possible theological or moral subversion. Melville had suffered astonishing losses: both of his sons, his early literary audience, his sense of any happiness whatsoever in a tormented life. Nearing the end, he was in no way reconciled, whether with God or men, but he had transcended the need to cry out against the darkness. The story of the innocent Billy, the noble Captain Vere, and the wretched Claggart is so simple in its design as to seem an allegory, but the allegorizations of the interpreters of *Billy Budd* are unpersuasive. There is little that is Christ-like about Billy, Vere is hardly a Jehovah, and Claggart does not merit the bad eminence of being compared to Satan or to Iago. Melville so tells the story as to make most of our interpretative temptations rather irrelevant. It is as though he anticipated Kafka, who frequently wrote deliberately to confound interpretation. Borges was the first, I believe, to find in Melville one of the precursors of Franz Kafka, rightly locating the Kafkan vision particularly in the tale "Bartleby the Scrivener."

As opposed to *Billy Budd,* there does seem to be a strong autobiographical allegory in "Bartleby," whose stubborn resistance relates to Melville's own refusal to go on writing what the world expected of him and was willing to purchase. "I would prefer not to" is at once Bartleby's and Melville's stance, somewhat akin to Groucho Marx's "Whatever it is, I'm against it!" But the link between Bartleby the scrivener and Melville the writer, while profoundly suggestive, only begins the intricate labyrinth of meanings that the reader is free to traverse. "Bartleby the Scrivener," like such Kafkan parables as "The Great Wall of China" and "The Hunter Gracchus," scarcely can be circumscribed by endless interpretations. Curiously, "Bartleby" is the inverse of *Billy Budd,* since the art of that short novel is to suggest that interpretation is unnecessary. In "Bartleby" the hint is that interpretation is an authentic obligation, but one that cannot be fulfilled by any particular attempt.

With "Benito Cereno," we are suspended halfway between the deceptive simplicity of *Billy Budd* and the seductive opacity of "Bartleby the Scrivener." In the celebrated exchange between Captain Delano's "you are saved: what has cast such a shadow upon you," and Benito Cereno's response, "the negro," a rather equivocal space for interpretation seems first to open wide, and then closes itself off again. Captain Vere and Billy Budd achieve so close a complicity as to form a kind of spiritual union, one that can save neither of them. The lawyer-narrator of "Bartleby the Scrivener" and poor Bartleby are so divided that we can muse upon their dialectical complicity, in an endless tension. But the complicity (if it exists) of Benito Cereno and Captain Delano is of another order, one that ambiguously seems both to unite and divide them. Are they opposed in their deepest natures, or are they secret sharers in each other's guilt? Melville allows us either option of interpretation and perhaps gives us no guidance between the two. ❖

Biography of Herman Melville

Herman Melville was born in New York City on August 1, 1819, to Allan and Maria Gansevoort Melville. Both his grand-fathers had served with distinction in the American Revolution, and his father headed a profitable import business. In 1830, however, financial troubles forced the family to move to Albany, and two years later Allan Melville died. After attending the Albany Academy, Herman Melville worked in a bank, on his uncle's farm, and in his brother's fur store. The family had to move once again, this time to the small town of Lansingburgh, outside of Albany, when the depression of 1837 bankrupted Melville's brother. For a short time, Melville taught at a country school and studied surveying in hopes of obtaining work on the Erie Canal building project.

To escape the bleak prospects at home, Melville joined the crew of a packet boat sailing for Liverpool, England, in 1839. Following another brief teaching stint, he left Fairhaven, Massachusetts, in January 1841 on the whaling ship *Acushnet*. A year and a half later, he and a friend acted on their boredom and discontent and deserted the ship at Nuku Hiva in the Marquesas Islands. He spent a few weeks with the Typee, who were rumored to be cannibals, until escaping on the whaling ship *Lucy Ann*. After being jailed in Tahiti for mutiny, he sailed to Honolulu, Hawaii. Finally, in August 1843, he joined the U.S. Navy to sail home on the frigate *United States* and was honor-ably discharged in Boston in October 1844.

Back home in Lansingburgh, Melville was encouraged by family and friends to write down his adventures. He read some books to expand his knowledge of the geography and ethnog-raphy of the South Seas and then composed *Typee,* an account of his time in the Marquesas Islands. The book, which was billed as nonfiction, was published in England and America in 1846. Its sequel, *Omoo,* debuted in 1847, and both volumes earned accolades with critics and the public.

Melville decided to pursue writing as a career and settled in New York City. In 1847, he married Elizabeth Shaw, the daughter of Massachusetts Supreme Court chief justice Lemuel Shaw, and soon started a family; the couple had two sons and two daughters. In 1849, he published *Mardi,* a sea story laden with allegory and symbolism, to great disappointment. Trying to regain his audience, Melville set aside his philosophical leanings to write the straightforward adventure tales *Redburn* (1849) and *White-Jacket* (1850). He drew upon memories of his first disheartening voyage to Liverpool to write the former and used his naval experience to depict life on a man-of-war in the latter.

After moving with his family to a farm near Pittsfield, Massachusetts, Melville once again concentrated on expressing himself fully. He developed a friendship with fellow author Nathaniel Hawthorne, who provided support while Melville undertook his most ambitious work, *Moby-Dick; or, The Whale.* Though the novel failed dismally upon its publication in 1851, it has since been heralded as a masterpiece of American literature. The story of Captain Ahab's obsessive quest to kill his cetacean nemesis, *Moby-Dick* blends a gripping adventure narrative, technical details of the whaling industry, and vivid characterizations with symbolism and deeply layered philosophical themes.

Although these were the most creatively productive years of his life, they may also have been the most difficult. The public rejection of *Moby-Dick* deeply depressed him. Struggling to support his wife and children on the farm, he had to borrow money from family members. To earn extra income, he wrote short stories for *Putnam's* and *Harper's* magazines. In 1852, he suffered another disappointment with the tragedy *Pierre,* an early psychological novel about a poet trying to be virtuous in the face of moral ambiguity. *Israel Potter* (1855), first serialized in *Putnam's,* concerned the apathetic treatment of a Revolutionary War veteran. His magazine pieces were collected in *The Piazza Tales* in 1856; they included "The Encantadas," about the Galapagos Islands, "Benito Cereno" (*Putnam's,* October 1855), about a slave ship rebellion, and "Bartleby the Scrivener" (*Putnam's,* November 1853), about a mysteriously recalcitrant clerk. In 1857, he published *The Confidence-Man,* a sardonic allegory on American manners.

Faced with the continued poor reception of his work, Melville gave up writing for a living. From 1856 to 1857, his father-in-law financed a trip to Europe and the Holy Land in the hope that it would alleviate his depression. Melville kept a diary of his journey, which was published in 1935 as *Journal Up the Straits,* and made the lecture circuit when he returned to the United States. In 1860, he embarked on his last sea voyage, sailing to San Francisco on a clipper ship owned by one of his brothers. Melville sold his farm in 1863 and returned to New York, where he worked as a customs inspector from 1866 until 1885.

During these years, he continued to write for pleasure. In 1866, he published his first volume of poetry, *Battle-Pieces and Aspects of the War,* which focused on the Civil War. *Clarel,* a long philosophical poem about a group of pilgrims in the Holy Land, followed in 1876. Two privately printed poetry collections, *John Marr and Other Sailors* and *Timoleon,* appeared toward the end of his life. Although his poetry has been dismissed by critics, the short novel he wrote sporadically between 1888 and 1891, *Billy Budd* (first published in 1924 in Volume 13 of the Standard Edition of his *Works*), has earned acclaim for its stirring depiction of arbitrary justice on a man-of-war.

Melville died in New York City on September 28, 1891. His death passed nearly unnoticed, and the brief obituaries marking it remembered *Typee* as his best book. However, Melville's work was rediscovered after World War I and has been receiving appreciative attention ever since. ❖

Thematic and Structural Analysis

In "Bartleby the Scrivener," "Benito Cereno," and *Billy Budd,* Herman Melville offers representations of law and legal systems: the lawyer who employs Bartleby and the legal process that imprisons him; Cereno's testimony to a Peruvian court; and the shipboard court that tries Billy Budd. Although one could say that the law triumphs in "Benito Cereno," in the other stories the legal system seems powerful but flawed—unable to deal with the enigmatic and contradictory natures of Bartleby and Billy Budd. All three stories are also to some degree about interpretation, about trying to "read" situations and people to reach a clear meaning, yet at the same time they suggest the impossibility of ever knowing the truth.

"Bartleby the Scrivener"

The story opens with the narrator introducing himself, although he neglects to tell us his name. An elderly, prudent, and "unambitious" lawyer who works on Wall Street, the narrator eschews courtrooms and trials in favor of the law's financial aspects—"rich men's bonds, and mortgages, and title deeds." He tells us that at the time his story begins—he is narrating past events—he had just been appointed to the office of master in chancery, a "pleasantly remunerative" but not arduous position.

The narrator describes his former office on Wall Street, which, fittingly, was almost walled in—the windows at one end of the office looking out onto a white wall, and at the other end, onto a black wall. The lawyer comments that the view from the office is "deficient in what landscape painters call 'life.' "

The lawyer employs two scriveners to copy the various legal documents that he prepares and an office boy; with the names Turkey, Nippers, and Ginger Nut, the employees seem to have wandered in from a Dickens novel. After being appointed to the chancery position, the lawyer hires an additional copyist, Bartleby, whose behavior presents a marked contrast to the other three employees, in spite of their pronounced idiosyncrasies. Indeed, at the beginning of the story the lawyer says that Bartleby is the "strangest scrivener I ever saw or heard of."

Initially Bartleby seems to fit in, sitting quietly outside the lawyer's inner office at a desk beside a window with "no view at all." Bartleby embarks on a frenzy of writing: "As if long famishing for something to copy, he seemed to gorge himself on my documents," says the narrator. The first glimmer of Bartleby's strangeness comes when he refuses to check his copies for accuracy, saying, "I would prefer not to." A few days later, Bartleby again refuses to read aloud copy to check it, this time in front of the other employees, again saying simply, "I would prefer not to." Over the next few days, the lawyer ponders whether he should dismiss the scrivener but eventually decides to indulge Bartleby's peculiarity, although not out of a sense of compassion: "Here I can cheaply purchase a delicious self-approval. . . . To befriend Bartleby, to humor him in his strange willfulness, will cost me little or nothing, while I lay up in my soul what will eventually prove a sweet morsel for my conscience." As if to demonstrate the pervasiveness of Wall Street's economics and its doctrine of self-interest, even acts of kindness become financial transactions that benefit the soul.

Matters continue in this way for some time, with the lawyer trying to tolerate Bartleby's refusals, but feeling "strangely goaded" to elicit some sort of response from the scrivener. However, the lawyer begins to reconcile himself to and even appreciate Bartleby's habits, noticing that "*he was always there.*" One Sunday, when the lawyer unexpectedly decides to drop by his office, the door is opened from within by Bartleby, who tells the lawyer that he would prefer not to let him in at the moment and suggests that he return after walking around the block, by which time Bartleby will have "concluded his affairs." The disconcerted lawyer follows his employee's directions, but when he returns Bartleby is gone. Upon further exploration, he realizes that "for an indefinite period Bartleby must have ate, dressed, and slept in [his] office, and that, too without plate, mirror, or bed." Peering into the scrivener's desk, he sees a knotted handkerchief—Bartleby's "savings bank," which seems to contain the sum of the copyist's worldly goods.

Instead of being angry, the lawyer is moved; he feels a "bond of common humanity. . . . [a] fraternal melancholy!" He pities Bartleby's loneliness, reflecting on the scrivener's seemingly self-imposed isolation. However, as he recollects Bartleby's habit of standing, "looking out, at his pale window behind the screen, upon the dead brick wall," his compassionate feelings change to fear and repulsion. The narrator reflects that although "up to a certain point . . . misery enlists our best affections . . . beyond that point we lose our capacity to pity." When faced with the "certain hopelessness of remedying excessive and organic ill," we begin to lose our compassion. To the lawyer, Bartleby presents such a case; he reflects, "I might give alms to his body; but his body did not pain him; it was his soul that suffered, and his soul I could not reach." He decides to dismiss Bartleby from service if the clerk cannot justify his actions.

However, Bartleby will not answer the lawyer's questions and, after another week or so, announces that he has "given up copying." This is the last straw for the lawyer, who, though sorry, gives Bartleby six days' notice. On the sixth day the lawyer leaves Bartleby his wages and tells the scrivener he must go, to which Bartleby answers, "I would prefer not." However, the lawyer goes home, simply assuming that by the next morning Bartleby and the money will be gone. The next day, though, he realizes that Bartleby is "more a man of preferences than assumptions." And indeed, when the lawyer opens the door of his office, he hears Bartleby say, "Not yet; I am occupied." The lawyer's "doctrine of assumption" has clearly failed, and, stymied by Bartleby's admonition, he gives up. Remarking that "charity often operates as a vastly wise and prudent principle—a great safeguard to its possessor," he decides to try to accept the mystery presented by Bartleby and his "dead-wall reveries." Choosing the laws of altruism over those of capitalism, the lawyer lets the nonproductive Bartleby remain.

However, as Bartleby's presence becomes a scandal on Wall Street, pressure from acquaintances forces the lawyer to again ask Bartleby to leave, but again Bartleby refuses. In desperation the lawyer decides that if Bartleby will not quit the office, then he himself will. He moves the location of his office and leaves Bartleby standing at a window in the empty room. At this point, the problem presented by Bartleby shifts from being an economic one (an employee who breaks the laws of capitalism by refusing to work) to a legal one (trespassing).

When Bartleby refuses to leave the building even after the new tenants have evicted him, they ask the lawyer for help, and he eventually agrees to talk to Bartleby, presenting him with a number of job opportunities. He even asks the scrivener to "go home with [him] now . . . and remain there till [they] can conclude upon some convenient arrangement." This offer represents the apogee of the lawyer's movement away from financial self-interest, but Bartleby refuses: "No: at present I would prefer not to make any change at all."

The lawyer flees the city, almost maddened by Bartleby's inscrutability, and the new tenants have Bartleby jailed in New York's Halls of Justice, also known as the Tombs. On his return, the lawyer asks the courts to be compassionate to Bartleby and then visits him in prison. There he finds Bartleby standing in the prison yard facing a wall. He refuses the lawyer's help, including offers of food, and the next time the lawyer comes to visit, Bartleby is lying dead on the ground, "huddled at the base of the wall."

The story ends here, except for one paragraph that reports a rumor the lawyer heard that Bartleby had previously worked at the Dead Letter Office in Washington. To the lawyer, the Dead Letter Office suggests "dead men." He asks his readers to imagine what such work—sorting and burning these undeliverable and unreturnable letters—would have done to a man already "prone to a pallid hopelessness." He imagines the contents of these letters, "pardon for those who died despairing; hope for those who died unhoping. . . . On errands of life, these letters sped to death." Moved by this thought, he exclaims, "Ah, Bartleby! Ah humanity!" With this final yoking of Bartleby to the world, the narrative of the inscrutable scrivener comes to a close.

These dead letters connect the reader to the repeated images of Bartleby in one of his "dead-wall reveries." It does not matter to Bartleby whether he stares at a wall on Wall Street or a prison wall, whether he is entombed in the lawyer's office or in the Tombs; the only escape from either is death. There is no thinking or communication in Bartleby's world: The dead letters communicate with no one, and as a scrivener he is only copying what has already been written. Even the attempts of the narrator, perhaps the only thinking person in the story, to solve the mystery posed by Bartleby are foiled by Bartleby's intransigence.

"Benito Cereno"

Melville's long short story of intrigue aboard a slave ship is based on actual events recorded by the real-life Captain Amasa Delano in his *Narrative of Voyages and Travels in the Northern and Southern Hemisphere* (1817). However, Melville's story alters the account, setting the action in 1799, six years earlier than its 1805 date, and changing the name of the ship. These alterations place the issues of slavery and racism squarely at the center of Melville's text, for the story takes place shortly after the slave revolt in San Domingo (Haiti), an allusion signalled by Melville's name for the ship, the *San Dominick*. When the story was published in 1855, national discussions about extending slavery throughout new territories were at a fever pitch—making the altered focus even more timely. Audiences would also have had on their minds the slave uprising led by Nat Turner in 1831, the same year that slaves in British Jamaica were emancipated.

The story opens with Captain Amasa Delano's ship, *Bachelor's Delight*, at anchor in the harbor of the uninhabited St. Maria Island off the Chilean coast. Captain Delano, who hails from Duxbury, Massachusetts, is much like the lawyer of "Bartleby," a man sure of his own goodness, who relies on the world to present itself in a rational and intelligible manner. When a Spanish ship, a merchantman in great disrepair, sails into view, Delano rows out to offer his aid.

As Delano climbs aboard the decaying ship, he is surrounded by a crowd of both blacks and whites—the vessel being a slaver or a "negro transportation" craft. Delano notices that there are more blacks than whites, and that on the poop deck sit six black men polishing rusty hatchets. Melville writes that to climb aboard a strange ship is like "entering a strange house with strange inmates in a strange land." A ship hides its contents from view until the last moment, when it suddenly discloses "the living spectacle it contains" to create "a shadowy tableau just emerged from the deep." The tension of the story arises from Delano's efforts to understand the nature of the "shadowy tableau" presented by the San Dominick, something he cannot do until the end of the story, when the inadequacy of his perception is revealed.

The captain of the ship, Don Benito Cereno, greets Delano and is accompanied by a small black man, Babo, whom Delano assumes is the captain's slave. Cereno is a pale Spaniard who seems to be suffering both physically and mentally, and Delano is pleased to see that Babo cares for him as devotedly as "a shepherd's dog." But Cereno treats Delano oddly, wavering between rudeness, warmth, arrogance, and gratitude. The American notices the ship's disarray, noisiness, and seeming absence of officers, attributing these problems to Cereno's poor leadership. At Delano's insistence, Cereno explains what has befallen his ship, occasionally breaking down to weep and cough.

Cereno tells Delano that the San Dominick, which had left Buenos Aires more than six months before, was hit by heavy storm that swept men overboard and damaged the ship. Scurvy and fever then broke out, and supplies ran low; with almost all the officers dead, the ship was left to drift. During the course of the story, Cereno frequently interrupts himself to praise Babo as the man to whom he owes "not only [his] own preservation, but likewise . . . the merit . . . of pacifying his more ignorant brethren." Delano is moved by the "beauty of that relationship which could present such a spectacle of fidelity on the one hand and confidence on the other." Delano, pitying Cereno, who he is now certain received his post through family connections, tells the Spaniard that he will help him to reach the nearest port.

As Delano moves about the ship, he grows uneasy. He has to walk between the row of men polishing hatchets and sees a black boy, enraged by a comment, strike a Spanish boy on the head with a knife. When Delano asks about the incident, which indicates to him an unthinkable lack of discipline, Cereno shrugs. Delano rationalizes the event to himself, as he does with every strange occurrence throughout the story, by attributing it to Cereno's unbalanced mind and poor leadership abilities. Meanwhile, Cereno tells Delano about the death from fever of his close friend Alexandro Aranda, who was also the owner of the slaves.

The next odd vision that presents itself is the figure of the giant slave, Atufal, who is marched, wrapped in chains, to stand before Cereno. The Spaniard demands that he ask for pardon, but Atufal refuses. Cereno sends him away and explains to Delano that Atufal has committed a dire offense and as punishment has been brought every two hours for the last sixty days to beg Cereno's pardon but has refused to do so. When Delano praises Atufal's "royal spirit," Cereno tells him that the slave was a king in Africa. Babo points out that while Atufal carries the padlock, the key is around Cereno's neck; to be freed, Atufal must simply "ask master's pardon." Delano thinks that perhaps Atufal does not need such an extreme punishment and finds himself a little annoyed at Babo's "conversational familiarities," wondering also at the "secret vindictiveness of the morbidly sensitive Spaniard."

After Atufal withdraws, Babo and Cereno move to another section of the deck, where they stand whispering. Cereno returns to ask Delano about his ship's cargo, the number of men aboard, and whether the ship is armed, making Delano uneasy. Cereno and his slave retreat again, abandoning Delano, who, disconcerted, wanders the deck, hearing the blacks still polishing their hatchets and watching a young Spanish sailor stare fixedly at the whispering men. Delano begins to wonder if perhaps the men are plotting something but reflects that if "Don Benito's story was, throughout, an invention, then every soul on board . . . was his carefully drilled recruit in the plot: an incredible inference." Laughing to himself at this impossibility—thinking the Africans "too stupid" for such a scheme—he continues walking the deck.

All the sailors Delano sees are accompanied by several Africans, who help them with their chores. Delano approaches an old sailor who is tying a knot and asks what the knot is for; the old man replies, "[F]or someone else to undo," and tosses the knot to Delano, muttering in broken English (rather than the Spanish spoken elsewhere on the ship), "Undo it, cut it, quick." Delano stands there, "knot in hand and knot in head," while the old sailor, followed by his black helpers, disappears to the front of the ship. The oddity of the situation makes Delano uneasy, but when he sees his whaleboat, *Rover,* approaching, he regains his confidence: "I to be murdered here at the ends of the earth on board a haunted pirate ship by a horrible Spaniard? Too nonsensical to believe! Who would kill Amasa Delano? His conscience is clean."

Delano helps distribute supplies and then is invited by Babo and Cereno to continue their discussion while Babo shaves Cereno, a luxury Delano find peculiar given the dire straits of the ship. He observes that "most Negroes are natural valets and hairdressers . . . [they have] a certain easy cheerfulness . . . as though God had set the whole Negro to some pleasant tune." The shaving scene appears to Delano as an example of "the African love of . . . fine shows," particularly the flourish with which Babo tucks a piece of brightly colored bunting under Cereno's chin. However, when the bunting falls to the floor, Delano realizes that it is the Spanish flag. which Cereno feebly laughs off as a joke. For a moment Delano has the impression, as Babo lifts the razor, "that in the black he saw a headsman, and in the white a man at the block." However, he shakes it off and listens to Cereno tell more of his story, all the while admiring Babo's skill.

At lunch, however, Delano wishes that Babo would leave the captains alone, but Cereno refuses to dismiss his attendant. Delano thinks this peculiar but no more so than anything else. After lunch the breeze picks up, and Delano begins to prepare to return to his own ship. He invites Cereno back to the *Bachelor's Delight* once the two ships are joined together, but Cereno bluntly refuses. Again his behavior puzzles Delano and makes him wonder if the Spaniard is plotting against him; as he walks up to the deck past Atufal, he wonders if the man is going to kill him at Cereno's orders. However, Delano makes it unharmed to the side of the ship, where Cereno bids him an almost tearful farewell: "Adieu, my dear, dear Don Amasa."

Delano descends to his boat, but, as the sailors begin to row away, Cereno suddenly flings himself into the boat and Spanish sailors hurl themselves overboard. Delano seizes Cereno by the throat, calling out that "this plotting pirate means murder!" At that instant, Babo, armed with a dagger, also jumps into the boat. He is soon disarmed, but suddenly a sailor yells a warning—Babo, pulling out a hidden knife, is "snakishly writhing up from the boat's bottom at the heart of his master, his countenance lividly vindictive." As Delano finally realizes what has been going on aboard the *San Dominick,* the canvas covering its figurehead drops away, revealing a human skeleton and the phrase "Follow your leader" written beneath it. The skeleton is that of Cereno's friend Alexandro Aranda, in reality killed by the mutinous slaves.

A fight ensues between the slaves and Delano's sailors, to whom Delano promises money if they capture the mutineers. The slaves are defeated, and the two ships sail to Lima, where Cereno is hospitalized and a hearing takes place.

At this point the text switches from a third-person narrative to a deposition—Cereno's written testimony about the events on his ship. Although Melville tells us that Cereno's account was first dismissed as that of a madman—no one able to believe slaves capable of such a plot—the subsequent testimony of other sailors confirmed his tale. Through the deposition we learn the truth behind Delano's perceptions; the document is the "key to fit into the lock of the complications which precede it."

The deposition begins with the *San Dominick'*s departure from Valparaiso with a cargo of 160 slaves, mostly belonging to Alexandro Aranda. A week into the voyage, the slaves, led by Babo and Atufal, launched a mutiny, killing most of the ship's whites but ordering Cereno to sail the ship to Senegal. To gain time, Cereno told the slaves that he had to take on water before the voyage and sailed around the South American coast, hoping to meet another vessel. During this period, the slaves killed Aranda, who became a grisly reminder to the whites of the consequences of rebellion—his skeleton was "substituted for the ship's proper figure-head . . . Christopher Colon, the discoverer of the New World," with Babo warning,

"Keep faith with the blacks from here to Senegal, or you shall in spirit, as now in body, follow your leader." In order to assure the safety of the remaining whites, Cereno agreed to enter into a contract with the slaves that guaranteed that Cereno would take them to Senegal and legally make over the ship to them, while the slaves, in turn, agreed not to kill anymore—an interesting twist on Melville's concern with law and justice.

The text skips over the details of the "prolonged and perplexed navigation" to the day the San Dominick arrived at St. Maria and spotted the Bachelor's Delight. The deposition then presents the truth behind the subterfuge that Delano witnessed. The hatchet polishers were ready to distribute weapons at a moment's notice, and Atufal's presence served as a warning to Cereno not to deviate from his script. Atufal wanted to kill Delano while he was aboard the San Dominick, while Babo intended to steal aboard the American ship, kill the crew, and force Delano to sail them to Senegal after the ships were yoked together. Ironically, Delano perceived the existence of a plot but could not bring himself to believe it, thinking blacks incapable of concocting or even participating in such a scheme. The deposition then describes Cereno's escape, the ensuing battle, and the capture of the San Dominick, ending with the decision of Cereno, who is "broken in body and mind," to retire to a monastery.

The story's conclusion, its third and briefest section, jumps backward in time to the two ships' voyage to Lima after the capture of the San Dominick, with Melville noting that the "nature of this narrative" necessitates the story's mixed-up sequence of events. On board the Bachelor's Delight, Cereno gently chides Delano for doubting his character: "[Y]our last act was to clutch me for a monster, not only an innocent man, but the most pitiable of all men." He reflects, "So far may even the best man err, in judging the conduct of one with the recesses of whose condition he is not acquainted." Indeed, Delano's misreading is at the heart of the story; unable to believe "negroes" capable of concocting a plot, he made Cereno the focus of his suspicions. However, his own disinclination to think or judge anyone as evil—even a slaveholder—made it impossible for him to trust the ominous warnings he received on the ship.

While the law in "Benito Cereno" seems to mete out justice—punishing the mutineers—the story forces us to examine the ways in which slavery demonizes all of those involved. Delano's blithe ability to forget what has happened—he tells Cereno, "Forget it. See, yon bright sun has forgotten it all, and the blue sea . . . these have turned over new leaves"—suggests that, despite being a Yankee and almost falling victim to rebelling slaves, he does not find slavery evil. However, Cereno is unable to put events behind himself. When Delano asks, "[Y]ou are saved: what has cast such a shadow upon you?" Cereno answers, "The negro." Indeed, even in death Cereno seems unable to escape. After Babo is executed, his head is placed on a pole in a plaza where his eyes

> met, unabashed, the gaze of the whites; and . . . looked towards St. Bartholomew's church, in whose vault slept then, as now, the recovered bones of Aranda . . . [and] towards the monastery . . . where, three months after being dismissed by the court, Benito Cereno, borne on a bier, did, indeed, follow his leader.

Billy Budd

Melville's novella *Billy Budd, Sailor (An Inside Narrative)* begins in "the time before steamships" with a description of the figure of the "Handsome Sailor," whose qualities are embodied in the title character, Billy Budd. The unnamed narrator, who periodically deviates from the story to offer his own thoughts and experiences, describes this type as characterized by a combination of strength and beauty. Inspiring the homage of his fellow shipmen, the Handsome Sailor's "moral nature was very seldom out of keeping with his physical make."

We first see Billy, a sailor aboard the merchantman *Rights-of-Man,* being impressed into service aboard the British man-of-war *Bellipotent* (or, in some editions, *Indomitable*). While Billy does not object, his captain, Graveling, laments at losing the sailor whose sweet disposition has brought harmony to his once-discordant ship. However, Billy is still impressed and, as he is being rowed to the *Bellipotent,* bids his ship farewell with the eerily prophetic words: "And good-bye to you, too, old *Rights-of-Man.*"

As Billy adjusts to naval life, we learn that he is an anomaly aboard the vessel. Almost preternaturally innocent and guileless, Billy is unable to "deal with double meanings and insinuations of any sort." Although a foundling, his strong physique and fine features indicate a noble lineage. Comparing Billy to Adam, Melville suggests that the sailor possesses a kind of virtue that predates, and is in fact antithetical to, civilization. However, Billy does have one flaw—he stutters severely under duress—an "imperfection" that the narrator declares proves that this story is "no romance."

The narrator then tells us that the year is 1797 and the *Bellipotent* is on its way to join the British fleet in the Mediterranean. Earlier that year, Britain experienced the Nore Mutiny, which was referred to as the "Great Mutiny." The narrator muses on this event and tells his readers that he will "err" from his story on a "bypath"—the first of many such asides—to discuss naval warfare and the feats of Admiral Nelson. He ends his historical meditations by explaining that the mutiny left a legacy of "anxiety" and "precautionary vigilance against relapse."

Returning to the story, the narrator focuses upon the *Bellipotent*'s captain, the Honorable Edward Fairfax Vere, called "Starry Vere," a dignified, reserved, and bookish man whose "convictions [are] a dike against those invading waters of novel opinion, social, political, and otherwise." Possessing many "sterling qualities but no brilliant ones," Vere is strict, yet just.

Melville then focuses on the third of the novella's central characters, John Claggart, nicknamed Jemmy Legs, who is a master-at-arms, "a sort of chief of police" in charge of maintaining order among the sailors. In contrast to Billy's tanned, rosy complexion, Claggart's pallor suggests "something defective or abnormal in the constitution and blood." However, his otherwise gentlemanly appearance belies this impression, and he appears to be "a man of high quality, social and moral, who for reasons of his own was keeping incog." His background is mysterious, and the narrator hints that Claggart may be a criminal sent to sea instead of prison.

A short while after his impressment, Billy, who has been assigned to the foretop, sees a young sailor flogged and vows never to break any rules. But inexplicably he keeps getting into trouble for minor infractions and asks a wily old sailor, Dansker, why. Dansker, who calls Billy "Baby Budd," cryptically tells him that Claggart "is down on him" and that he had better be careful. Billy does not believe this, because Claggart has always been pleasant to him. Billy cannot believe that appearances may be deceiving and even thinks he has disproved Dansker when he accidentally spills soup in front of Claggart, who says nothing except, "Handsomely done, my lad! And handsome is as handsome did it too!" Billy, not hearing Claggart's sarcasm, tells his shipmates, "There now, who says that Jemmy Legs is down on me!"

However, Claggart has indeed developed an antipathy for Billy, about which we learn in another aside. In Claggart, writes Melville, is "the mania of an evil nature . . . born with him and innate." The evil hides itself "in the mantle of respectability," allowing a man like Claggart to seem sane, although his hatred is completely divorced from reason, which it uses only as a tool to obtain its own irrational ends. The source of Claggart's hatred for Billy lies in Billy's "significant personal beauty" and the innocence it reflects—"a nature that . . . [has] in its simplicity never willed malice or experienced the reactionary bite of the serpent." So what recourse, the narrator asks, does a nature like Claggart's in turn have "but to recoil upon itself and, like the scorpion for which the Creator alone is responsible, act out to the end the part allotted it." Provoked by his hatred of Billy, Claggart interprets the spilled soup as a deliberate act of contempt, an idea confirmed by his henchman, Squeak, who has been making trouble for Billy while also misrepresenting his actions to Claggart. The narrator remarks, "But Claggart's conscience being but the lawyer to his will, made ogres out of trifles . . . [and] justified animosity into a sort of retributive righteousness."

Later, one of Claggart's minions summons Billy to a midnight meeting to plot a mutiny. Billy protests—stuttering badly as he always does under stress—and threatens to throw the plotter overboard. Although required by naval law to report such an incident, Billy, in a show of misguided honor, does not.

This incident leaves Billy deeply confused, "like a young horse fresh from the pasture suddenly inhaling a vile whiff from some chemical factory." When he reports the incident to Dansker, the old man repeats his warning that "*Jemmy Legs* is *down*" on Billy, which Billy again ignores because of Claggart's friendly demeanor. Meanwhile, Billy has stopped getting into trouble, and Claggart's friendliness has become more pronounced. Melville writes that sometimes when Claggart watches Billy, his eyes fill with tears and his "melancholy expression [has] in it a touch of soft yearning, as if Claggart could [love] Billy but for fate and ban." However, Claggart's "monomania" continues to gnaw at him.

Claggart soon goes to Vere and tells him that the impressed men are plotting a mutiny, with Billy as their ringleader. When Vere questions this accusation, Claggart warns that beneath Billy's handsome and innocent appearance, which Vere likens to a "young Adam before the Fall," may lurk a traitor. When Billy is brought into Vere's cabin, Claggart repeats the charges, but Billy is so overwhelmed that he literally cannot speak, choking and gurgling. In desperation, Billy lashes out at Claggart, striking him in the forehead, and Claggart falls to the ground, dead. Vere whispers, "Fated boy . . . what have you done!" and the two struggle to remove Claggart's corpse, which is compared to a "dead snake."

Vere is left in a legal conundrum: He must decide how to handle this case in which the "innocence and guilt personified in Claggart and Budd in effect changed places." He believes Billy to have been falsely accused but realizes he has committed murder, a crime punishable by death. He sums up the problem: "Struck dead by an angel of God! Yet the angel must hang!"

To dispel any unrest a delay could cause, Vere decides to handle the problem immediately and convenes a drumhead court to hear the case. Billy and Vere both testify, but neither can attest to the cause of Claggart's hatred. Vere calls it "a matter for psychologic theologians to discuss" and asks, "But what is a military court to do with it? . . . The prisoner's deed—with that alone we have to do." After hearing the testimony, the men on the court are unable to make a decision, but Vere prods them in the correct legal direction, urging that they put aside all moral considerations in favor of martial law: "Our vowed responsibility is in this: That however pitilessly that law may operate, we nevertheless adhere to it and administer it. . . . But let not warm hearts betray heads that should be cool." They must follow the Mutiny Act, which, like its "father," war, "looks only to the frontage, the appearance." If Billy is not punished, the sailors may take that as a sign that they, too, can break the rules. The court decides that Billy should be hanged at dawn the next day.

Vere visits Billy to tell him the verdict, and his face when he leaves Billy's prison reflects the fact that "the condemned one suffered less than he who mainly had effected the condemnation." Billy, who has no fear of death, goes calmly to the gallows the following morning and is hanged in front of the entire crew, "a martyr to military discipline." Billy's final words are "God bless Captain Vere!" and as he is drawn upward by the noose, "the vapory fleece hanging low in the East was shot through with a soft glory as of the fleece of the Lamb of God." Billy's body does not jerk or move in any way, a phenomenon whose significance is much debated by the sailors: either a sign that he is blessed by God, or a scientific oddity, but in either case, remarkable.

The novella "ends" in four different ways. The first ending is with Billy's actual death. The second is with Vere's death after being wounded in an ocean battle; he dies with Billy's name on his lips, which reflects how deeply Billy has affected him. The third ending of the story is a report of Billy's execution in a navy newspaper. The newspaper gets the facts wrong, presenting Billy as a conniving mutineer and John Claggart as an innocent victim killed in the line of duty. This distortion, however, justifies the legal system that condemned Billy to death. In the fourth and final ending, Billy becomes a legend to other sailors, for whom a chip from the spar from which he was hanged becomes "as a piece of the Cross." The story closes with a ballad composed by sailors aboard the *Bellipotent*, "Billy in the Darbies." In it Billy becomes a kind of sailors' martyr whose last words, "I am sleepy, and the oozy weeds about me twist," come from beyond the grave. Billy does, in a manner of speaking, have the last word.

The story presents a series of reversals: The innocent man is a murderer and the evil man is an innocent victim; the legal system punishes a man who should not be punished; the ending of the story is not in fact the ending. The religious language of the story, which portrays Billy as an innocent angel and likens him to Adam and Christ, asks us to read allegorically, but in fact the reversals of good and evil prevent us from doing so. Instead we are faced with the fact that law and order, structures we believe in, fail to cope adequately with Billy's crime and Claggart's sin.

The legal conundrum presented by Bartleby is echoed to some degree by the legal knot of *Billy Budd,* although the problem of *Billy Budd* is that neither party is either guilty or innocent: Each is both guilty *and* innocent. The legal system in "Benito Cereno" seems to prevail, except for the nagging sense one has that the racism of Captain Amasa Delano and of the court itself goes unpunished. In all three stories the reader is unsettled by ambiguity; the stories and their characters invite multiple interpretations and refuse to be contained by any one simple truth. As *Billy Budd*'s narrator tells us, "I am not certain whether to know the world and to know human nature be not two distinct branches of knowledge, which while they may coexist in the same heart, yet in either may exist with little or nothing of the other." ✤

—Deborah Williams
Iona College

List of Characters

"Bartleby the Scrivener"

Bartleby is the passive scrivener, or copyist, whose calm statement "I would prefer not to" dismantles his employer's complacent worldview.

The lawyer is the unnamed narrator who is deeply affected by Bartleby's situation. By the end of the story, when Bartleby has died, the lawyer is a more compassionate, less materialistic man.

Turkey, Nippers, and *Ginger Nut* are the lawyer's three other employees whose peculiarities meld to allow them to function as a smoothly running machine: Turkey cannot work in the morning, while Nippers cannot work in the afternoon; Ginger Nut is the errand boy who brings them food.

"Benito Cereno"

Benito Cereno is captain of the *San Dominick,* the Spanish ship that is commandeered by its cargo of slaves. He is held captive by the slaves and ordered to sail the ship to Senegal.

Amasa Delano is a historical figure whose narrative Melville used as a model for the novella. Delano is a Yankee captain who goes to the aid of the ailing *San Dominick,* and it is through his eyes that we see most of the events aboard the ship. Cereno's deposition at the end of the story proves Delano's perceptions to be inaccurate.

Alexandro Aranda, Cereno's friend and the owner of the slaves, is killed by the slaves before the story begins. His skeleton is installed as the slave ship's new figurehead, an emblem of the mutiny that has taken place.

Babo is the slave who masterminded the mutiny. Delano sees him as Cereno's slave—when in fact Cereno is Babo's prisoner.

Atufal is Babo's coconspirator. Although he is presented in chains aboard the *San Dominick,* this is in fact a warning to Cereno to keep the mutineers' secret.

Billy Budd

Billy Budd is the "Handsome Sailor" whose beauty draws the ill will of John Claggart. When Billy unintentionally kills Claggart, he is hanged and becomes a legend among other sailors.

John Claggart, the master-at-arms aboard the *Bellipotent,* is as evil as Billy is good. He schemes to frame Billy for plotting a mutiny and is killed by Billy when he accuses the sailor of being a mutineer.

Captain Vere, the captain of the *Bellipotent,* is the man responsible for ensuring that the law punishes Billy for his crime. While he believes that Billy has been victimized by Claggart, he feels that he must uphold the law at all costs.

Dansker is an old sailor aboard the *Bellipotent* who warns Billy that Claggart is after him. However, Billy does not believe him. ✤

Critical Views

[Raymond Weaver (1888–1948) was a literary critic and Melville scholar who wrote *Herman Melville: Mariner and Mystic* (1921) and was the first editor of *Billy Budd* when he included it in his edition of Melville's *Works* (1922–24). In this extract, Weaver argues that Melville wrote *Billy Budd* to illustrate the power of goodness and innocence over evil.]

Just as some theologians have presented the fall of man as evidence of the great glory of God, in similar manner Melville studies the evil in Claggart in vindication of the innocence in Billy Budd. For, primarily, Melville wrote *Billy Budd* in witness to his ultimate faith that evil is defeat and natural goodness invincible in the affections of man. *Billy Budd*, as *Pierre*, ends in disaster and death; in each case inexperience and innocence and seraphic impulse are wrecked against the malign forces of darkness that seem to preside over external human destiny. In *Pierre*, Melville had hurled himself into a fury of vituperation against the world; with *Billy Budd* he would justify the ways of God to man. Among the many parallels of contrast between these two books, each is a tragedy (as was Melville's life), but in opposed senses of the term. For tragedy may be viewed not as being essentially the representation of human misery, but rather as the representation of human goodness or nobility. All of the supremest art is tragic: but the tragedy is, in Aristotle's phrase, "the representation of Eudaimonia," or the highest kind of happiness. There is, of course, in this type of tragedy, with its essential quality of encouragement and triumph, no flinching of any horror of tragic life, no shirking of the truth by a feeble idealism, none of the compromises of the so-called "happy ending." The powers of evil and horror must be granted their fullest scope; it is only thus we can triumph over them. Even though in the end the tragic hero finds no friends among the living or dead, no help in God; only a deluge of calamity everywhere, yet in the very intensity of his affliction he may reveal the splendor undiscoverable in any gentler fate. Here he has

reached, not the bottom, but the crowning peak of fortune—
something which neither suffering nor misfortune can touch.
Only when worldly disaster has worked its utmost can we realize that there remains something in man's soul which is forever
beyond the grasp of the accidents of existence, with power in
its own right to make life beautiful. Only through tragedy of
this type could Melville affirm his everlasting yea. The final
great revelation—or great illusion—of his life, he uttered in
Billy Budd.

> —Raymond Weaver, "Introduction," *Shorter Novels of Herman
> Melville* by Herman Melville (New York: Liveright, 1928),
> pp. l–li

F. O. MATTHIESSEN ON TRAGEDY IN *BILLY BUDD*

[F. O. Matthiessen (1902–1950) was a prominent
scholar of Henry James and the author of *Henry James:
The Major Phase* (1944), *The American Novels of Henry
James* (1947), and *The Achievement of T. S. Eliot*
(1947). In this extract from his celebrated study of
nineteenth-century American literature, *American
Renaissance* (1941), Matthiessen comments on
Melville's concept of tragedy in *Billy Budd.*]

At the time of Captain Vere's announcement of Billy's sentence,
Melville remarked that it 'was listened to by the throng of
standing sailors in a dumbness like that of a seated congrega-
tion of believers in Hell listening to their clergyman's
announcement of his Calvinistic text.' At that point Melville
added in the margin of his manuscript the name of Jonathan
Edwards. The rectitude of Vere seems to have recalled to him
the inexorable logic, the tremendous force of mind in the
greatest of our theologians. Melville might also have reflected
that the relentless denial of the claims of ordinary nature on
which Edwards based his reasoned declaration of the absolute
Sovereignty of God had left its mark on the New England char-

acter, on such emotionally starved and one-sided figures as Hawthorne drew, on the nightmare of will which a perverted determinism had become in Ahab. Without minimizing the justice of Vere's stern mind, Melville could feel that the deepest need for rapaciously individualistic America was a radical affirmation of the heart. He knew that his conception of the young sailor's 'essential innocence' was in accord with no orthodoxy; but he found it 'an irruption of heretic thought hard to suppress.' The hardness was increased by his having also learned what Keats had, through his kindred apprehension of the meaning of Shakespeare, that the Heart is the Mind's Bible. Such knowledge was the source of the passionate humanity in Melville's own creation of tragedy.

How important it was to reaffirm the heart in the America in which *Billy Budd* was shaped can be corroborated by the search that was being made for the drift of significance in our eighteen-eighties and nineties by two of our most symptomatic minds. John Jay Chapman was already protesting against the conservative legalistic dryness that characterized our educated class, as fatal to real vitality; while Henry Adams, in assessing his heritage, knew that it tended too much towards the analytic mind, that it lacked juices. Those juices could spring only from the 'depth of tenderness,' the 'boundless sympathy' to which Adams responded in the symbol of the Virgin, but which Melville—for the phrases are his—had found in great tragedy. After all he had suffered Melville could endure to the end in the belief that though good goes to defeat and death, its radiance can redeem life. His career did not fall into what has been too often assumed to be the pattern for the lives of our artists: brilliant beginnings without staying power, truncated and broken by our hostile environment. Melville's endurance is a challenge for a later America.

—F. O. Matthiessen, "Billy Budd, Foretopman," *American Renaissance: Art and Expression in the Age of Emerson and Whitman* (New York: Oxford University Press, 1941), pp. 513–14

[Richard Chase (1914–1962) was a prominent American literary critic and the author of *Quest for Myth* (1949), *Walt Whitman Reconsidered* (1955), and *The American Novel and Its Tradition* (1957). In this extract from his book on Melville, Chase links the composition of "Bartleby the Scrivener" to the events in Melville's life, arguing that Melville was questioning the relationship between the artist and society.]

The short stories of this period of Melville's life are personal and introspective. Melville was thinking of himself as an artist and trying to understand the artist's relation to his society. Bearing this in mind and on the internal evidence of the story, there seems no doubt that Melville was consciously writing a parable of the artist in "Bartleby the Scrivener." The story is subtitled, "A Story of Wall Street." Bartleby is a scrivener—that is, a writer. He insists on writing only when moved to do so. Faced by the injunction of capitalist society that he write on demand, he refuses to compromise, and rather than write on demand writes not at all, devoting his energies to the task of surviving in his own way and on his own intransigent terms. The strained and complex relationship between Bartleby and the lawyer may have certain similarities to the relationship between Melville and his father-in-law, also a lawyer, who helped the Melville family finance itself while Melville went on writing instead of getting a job.

The other scriveners, Turkey and Nippers, represent what we might now call "middle-brow" culture. They have sold out to the commercial interests and suffer from the occupational diseases of the compromised artist in a commercial society—neurosis, alcoholism, and ulcers. Their depressions and manias are equally unproductive of first-rate work, and they maintain a grudging and suspicious attitude toward Bartleby, their acknowledged superior as a scrivener—the attitude of the uneasy middle-brow toward the genuine artist.

It was rumored that Bartleby had been "a subordinate clerk in the Dead Letter Office." That is, Melville, while he was still writing salable adventure stories and before his own intransigence began, with *Moby-Dick*, had been a minor practitioner in the moribund profession of letters. But he had lost his audience and these early writings were as dead as modern literature as a whole seemed to be. Bartleby had suddenly been removed from the Dead Letter Office "by a change of administration." "When I think over this rumor," writes the lawyer, "I cannot adequately express the emotions which seize me." No wonder, if this "change of administration" is a reference to the spiritual wager which removed Melville from New York to Pittsfield in order that he might start on the great work of his life. The last words of the story are, "On errands of life, these letters speed to death." For Melville, literature was life; ideally "Bartleby" should have been able to convey its message of love and vitality to the readers who awaited it. But there were no such readers—at least none such as might rescue Melville's fiction from the death he accurately predicted for it. "Ah Bartleby! Ah humanity!" The artist and the rest of mankind seemed to be fatally sundered.

But there is a profounder level of symbolic meaning in "Bartleby the Scrivener." Melville identifies himself partly with the lawyer. For example, when the lawyer describes himself complacently as "one of those unambitious lawyers who never addresses a jury, or in any way draws down public applause," the lawyer's complacency is certainly an irony, for Melville himself was by no means complacent about his lack of public applause. The lawyer tells us that he once had a lucrative position but lost it unexpectedly and along with it the income he expected would be lifelong—a reference presumably to the paying audience Melville commanded with his early books and then lost. And surely the lawyer's "original business—that of a conveyancer and title hunter, and drawer-up of recondite documents of all sorts" is a facetious reference to Melville's own business.

—Richard Chase, *Herman Melville: A Critical Study* (New York: Macmillan, 1949), pp. 146–48

NEWTON ARVIN ON "BENITO CERENO" AS ARTISTIC MISCARRIAGE

[Newton Arvin (1900–1963) was a notable American critic. Among his works are *Hawthorne* (1929), *Whitman* (1938), and *Longfellow: His Life and Work* (1962). In this extract from his book on Melville, Arvin asserts that the praise heaped on "Benito Cereno" is misdirected and that Melville wrote the tale with a lack of conviction.]

A far more ambitious and superficially more impressive narrative than "The Tartarus of Maids" is of course "Benito Cereno," the longest and most celebrated of the *Piazza Tales.* Unduly celebrated, surely. For neither the conception nor the actual composition and texture of "Benito" are of anything like the brilliance that has been repeatedly attributed to them. The story is an artistic miscarriage, with moments of undeniable power. It was a mistaken impulse this time that led Melville to rewrite another man's narrative; for, as everyone knows, the material of "Benito Cereno" was lifted bodily from a chapter in the *Narrative of Voyages and Travels* of a Yankee ship-captain named Amasa Delano. What Melville could do with the substance of other men's books, at his best, was magical, as we have already seen; but he largely fails to do this with Captain Delano's undecorated tale. Liberties, to be sure, he rather freely takes with his original, but strictly speaking he takes too few, and takes these too half-heartedly; and nothing is more expressive of the low pitch at which "Benito" is written than the fact that with one incident in his original Melville takes no liberties whatever: the scene of the actual mutiny on the *San Dominick,* which might have been transformed into an episode of great and frightful power, Melville was too tired to rewrite at all, and except for a few trifling details, he leaves it all as he found it, in the drearily prosaic prose of a judicial deposition.

Much praise has been lavished on the art with which an atmosphere of sinister foreboding and malign uncertainty is evoked and maintained through all the earlier parts of the tale. It is hard to see why. There are a few fine touches in the very first paragraphs—the "flights of troubled gray fowl," for example, skimming fitfully over the smooth waters like swallows over a meadow before a storm—but even in these first pages the rhythms of the prose are slow, torpid, and stiff-limbed; and they remain so, with a few moments of relief, throughout. Nor is the famous "atmosphere" of "Benito" created swiftly, boldly, and hypnotically, as Melville at his highest pitch might have created it; on the contrary, it is "built up" tediously and wastefully through the accumulation of incident upon incident, detail upon detail, as if to overwhelm the dullest-witted and most resistant reader. Many of the details, too, are of poor imaginative quality: the hatchet-polishers on the poop are rather comic than genuinely sinister; the symbolism of the key hanging round Don Benito's neck is painfully crude; and it needed only a very commonplace and magazinish inventiveness to conceive the scene in which Benito is shaved by the wily Babo. The traces of contrivance, and fatigued contrivance too, are visible everywhere in the story, and the sprinkling of clichés on every page—"a joyless mien," "the leaden calm," "fiends in human form," "a dark deed"—is only a verbal clue to the absence of strong conviction with which Melville is here writing.

—Newton Arvin, *Herman Melville* (New York: William Sloane Associates, 1950), pp 238–40

NORMAN HOLMES PEARSON ON EDWARD FAIRFAX VERE

[Norman Holmes Pearson (1909–1975) was a longtime professor of English at Yale University and the editor of *The Complete Novels and Selected Tales of Nathaniel Hawthorne* (1937). In this extract, Pearson explores the character of Edward Fairfax Vere in *Billy Budd*.]

The Honorable Edward Fairfax Vere was man as well as captain. He was *vir,* as Richard Chase suggests, as well as *veritas.* Unlike Billy, the apple of knowledge had been tasted by his lineage. His testing was of a different sort from Billy's, and of a kind closer to our own. Vere knew obedience, and for him reason was what Michael called "right Reason." Against this was the temptation of an allegiance to the heart and to the instincts, as Adam had bitten the fruit for love of Eve. To the original metaphor, Vere gives a new analogy as he reasons with the drumhead court to be firm.

> But the exceptional in the matter moves the heart within you. Even so too is mine moved. But let not warm hearts betray heads that should be cool. Ashore in a criminal case will an upright judge allow himself off the bench to be waylaid by some tender kinswoman of the accused seeking to touch him with her tearful plea? Well the heart sometimes the feminine in man, here is that piteous woman. And hard though it be, she must be ruled out.

This is the temptation which Eve represented, redacted upon the otherwise womanless *Indomitable*. This is the victory which the first Adam had not won. It is Vere alongside Billy. As Vere had paced his cabin before addressing the jury, he was "without knowing it symbolizing thus in his action a mind resolute to surmount difficulties even if against primitive instincts strong as the wind and the sea." It was as though he rejected the pattern of Ahab who had acted only on instinct, and had swept aside our sympathy for a primitivism which could no longer be based on innocence. Vere, as captain, was his majesty's responsible deputy in a world of fallen man.

As such Vere lived, doing with obedience all that should be done. Should he not then, this model of post-lapsarian man, have been rewarded with long years of life and an admiralcy? "On the return passage to the English fleet," Melville wrote, "from the detached cruise during which occurred the events already recorded, the *Indomitable* fell in with the *Athéiste*. An engagement ensued; during which Captain Vere, in the act of putting his ship alongside the enemy with a view of throwing his boarders across the bulwarks, was hit by a musket-ball from a port-hole of the enemy's main cabin." He died, but as he died

> he was heard to murmur words inexplicable to his attendant— "Billy Budd, Billy Budd." That these were not the accents of remorse, would seem clear from what the attendant said to the *Indomitable's* senior officer of marines. . . .

That Melville's third principal character in the story should have died with Billy's name on his lips, is as important to understand as the significance of mutiny or Vere's surmountal of temptation. For on it depends the ultimate tone of the book, without which there could be no final definition. Billy Budd's death may seem to indicate how hard is the path of the beatitudes when followed in life. His story summarized in "an authorized weekly publication" meant nothing but the malformation of episodes which comes with time, and especially for those "whose reading was mainly confined to the journals." For the common sailors the yarn was woven into a popular ballad, and for a time the spar from which he was hanged was divided into chips like pieces of the Cross. "They recalled the fresh young image of the Handsome Sailor, that face never deformed by a sneer or subtler vile freak of the heart within!" The event was within their experience, and they understood it the better for that. Theirs was the final average reaction, as Billy's example drifted into time. The example might help, but actually they would need the "peacemaker" again in the midst, whether on board the merchantman or the man-of-war. Certainly they would still require captaincy like Vere's.

Most of all, remembering the king's yarn of pedantry, we ourselves will recall Vere with whom we, like Melville, might most closely identify ourselves. Vere is like a Samson Agonistes, who, having conquered the temptation of the senses and remained true to the will and reason, is redeemed. But unlike Samson, Vere is not given the destruction of the French to serve as substitute for the tumbled temple. Yet Vere, though his ambitions were not satisfied, and the spirit of mutiny would appear again, was not without his consolation. As postlapsarian man, Vere has learned how to die, in his case by the example of a common sailor who was like a common carpenter. As the true Christian knows how to die in adversity with the peace which the name of Jesus brings to the lips, so "Billy Budd" is to Vere what "God bless Captain Vere" was to Budd. They were "not the words of remorse." Both to Billy Budd, and to Vere by Budd's example, is that joy and success of true captaincy of which Father Mapple had spoken to Ishmael and to us. "Delight—top-gallant delight is to him who acknowledges no law or lord but the Lord his God, and is only a patriot to heaven." Now, though the King of Kings was known chiefly by his rod, is that which Ahab never found through his disobedience and renunciation of true reason for the temptation of the instincts. There was no top-gallant delight for him, as there was for the captain of an *Indomitable* or for a Billy Budd who was in every sense a true foretopgallantman.

This is the responsible pattern for fallen man, constantly subject to mutiny and such events as, to return to Melville's woven strand of pedantry, "converted into irony for a time those spirited strains of Dibdin":

and as for my life, 'tis the King's!

"With mankind," Vere was accustomed to say, "forms, measured forms are everything; and that is the import couched in the story of Orpheus with his lyre spelling the wild denizens of the woods." "And this," as Melville states, "he once applied to the disruption of forms going across the Channel and the consequences thereof."
—Norman Holmes Pearson, "*Billy Budd*: The King's Yarn," *American Quarterly* 3, No. 2 (Summer 1951): 112–14

MILTON R. STERN ON BILLY BUDD'S SAINTLINESS

[Milton R. Stern (b. 1928) is Alumni Distinguished Professor of English at the University of Connecticut. He is the author of *The Golden Moment: The Novels of F. Scott Fitzgerald* (1970) and *Contests for Hawthorne: The Marble Faun and the Politics of Openness and Closure in American Literature* (1991). In this extract, Stern argues that Billy Budd possesses a Christ-like innocence.]

When Billy himself is presented, he too is the Handsome Sailor characterized by barbaric good humor, by a tall, athletic, symmetric figure, by the ability to box well, by proficiency in his calling, by a highly moral nature. The Handsome Sailor becomes the kind of innocent that the most attractive Typee savage is, and the repeated mention of Billy's barbarian innocence and his magnificent physical appearance predetermines the genre's essential mindlessness. Once more, the prehistoric and griefless Typee mindlessness is associated with the Edenic purity of Christian innocence. Billy is constantly presented as the prelapsarian Adam, indeed, one who "in the nude might have posed for a statue of young Adam before the fall." Melville repeatedly suggests that innocence, in the need for a knowledge of the history of the only world there is, is not a saving virtue, but a fatal flaw. The very goodness of Billy's ignorance of the world, while in accord with Christian teaching, becomes the sin of nonunderstanding, noncommunicating mindlessness marked by the stutter. Melville writes:

> In certain matters, some sailors even in mature life remain unsophisticated enough. But a young seafarer of the disposition of our athletic foretopman is much of a child-man. And yet a child's utter innocence is but its blank ignorance, and the innocence more or less wanes as intelligence waxes. But in Billy Budd, intelligence such as it was, had advanced, while yet his simple-mindedness remained for the most part unaffected. Experience is a teacher indeed; yet did Billy's years make his experience small. Besides he had none of that intuitive knowledge of the bad which in natures not good or incompletely so foreruns experience, and therefore may pertain, as in some instances it too clearly does pertain, even to youth.

The problem of Billy's mindlessness is not merely one of the Christ-like purity which is an absolute and predetermining absence of evil. The problem of Billy's mindlessness arises from his typically lure-like inexperience and inability to evaluate the experience he does have. Leaving no doubt at all about the nature of his rejection of ideal, Christly behavior, Melville sums up his statement about Billy by saying, "As it was, innocence was his blinder."

Billy, then, is particularized as the Adam-Christ within the general type of the Handsome Sailor: "Such a cynosure [the Handsome Sailor], at least in aspect, and something such too in nature, *though with important variations* made apparent as the story proceeds, was *welkin-eyed* Billy Budd or Baby Budd . . ." [italics mine]. Billy immediately is the beauty and childlike purity of the ideal. He is called both Beauty and Baby by his shipmates, and the detail of his "heaven-eyed" face occurs again and again. Even in the ever illuminating matter of origins (on the literal level, Billy's origins will turn out to be something quite different), Melville hints that Billy's unknown mother was one "eminently favored by Love and the Graces," and—who is his father? Well, "God knows, Sir." The Baby is not allowed to continue his straight and narrow path within the chronometrical and ideal sermon of the rights of man, but is born into the actualities of the Articles of War. "It was not very long prior to the time of the narration that follows that he had entered the King's service, having been impressed on the Narrow Seas from a homeward bound English merchantman [the *Rights of Man*] into a seventy-four outward-bound, *H.M.S. Indomitable.*" In *White-Jacket* Melville used the ship image precisely in the way it was to be used repeatedly in other books: the homeward bound ship is the ship bound to heaven, to something final and absolute. The outward bound ship, whether wrongly or rightly directed, is the actual state of the world, ever seeking, ever subject to the dark waters of new and unknown experiences, ever plowing new paths in the boundless waters of infinite relativity. In the actual world, Billy continues his behavior of ideal Christliness. Chronometrically and mindlessly he turns the other cheek to all new experiences, accepting everything with animal insightlessness and the childlike faith of innocence. "As to his enforced enlistment, that he seemed to take pretty much as he was wont to take any vicissitude of weather. Like the animals, though no philosopher, he was, without knowing it, practically a fatalist."

The ordinary, hard-working, Jarl-world of common gravelings depends upon Budd morality for the peaceful pursuits of an unarmed and productive world. When his merchant ship, the *Rights of Man,* is robbed of "man's earthly household peace" and "domestic felicity" by the arch-thief, the gun, Captain Graveling pleads with Lieutenant Ratcliffe lest the man-of-war remove the very possibility of a peaceful and moral world. "Ay, Lieutenant, you are going to take away the jewel of 'em; you are going to take away my peacemaker!" Immediately the Prince of Peace must be defined within the context of either the ideal, the Sermon and the *Rights of Man,* or hideous history, the Articles and the *Indomitable*. Immediately, first things come first, and the needs of the man-of-war world take precedence over the needs of the Ship of Peace. The bitterness of this story's irony and anger first becomes noticeable in the impressment scene. For Ratcliffe, who understands none of the things that Vere understands, and who can use the gun only in order to use the gun, makes the only possible, correct answer for all the wrong reasons: "Well," says he, "blessed are the peacemakers, especially the fighting peacemakers!" And pointing through the cabin window to the *Indomitable*, Ratcliffe adds, "And such are the seventy-four beauties some of which you see poking their noses out of the port-holes of yonder warship lying-to for me." For they, not the meek, inherit the earth.

—Milton R. Stern, *The Fine Hammered Steel of Herman Melville* (Urbana: University of Illinois Press, 1957), pp. 215–16

JAMES E. MILLER, JR., ON CAPTAIN VERE AS THE BALANCE BETWEEN HEART AND INTELLECT

[James E. Miller, Jr. (b. 1920), formerly a professor of English at the University of Chicago, is the author of many books, including *J. D. Salinger* (1965), *T. S. Eliot's Personal Wasteland* (1977), and *Walt Whitman* (1990). In this extract from his reader's guide to Melville, Miller investigates the character of Captain Vere in *Billy Budd*, finding him an ideal balance between heart and intellect.]

If Billy is the subtly masked man of innocence, appearing in the cloak of Christ's purity to the world and to himself while in reality harboring the savage impulse of the barbarian, the child, the animal; and if Claggart is the deceitfully masked man, deliberately and craftily misleading the world as to his true evil nature; then Captain Vere is Melville's maskless man, his man of forthrightness and frankness, who by his balance of reason and emotion, mind and heart, recognizes evil and its inevitability on earth, comes to honorable terms with it, and endures, albeit with a heightened tragic vision.

Captain Vere is a middle-aged Jack Chase or Rolfe, past their physical prime but exhibiting most of their fine qualities. As Billy Budd is a man of all heart and no intellect, and John Claggart a man of all intellect and no heart, Captain Vere is the man of moderation with heart and intellect in ideal balance. He is wise enough to refrain from "developing" his virtues to that extreme at which they become vices. He is mindful of the welfare of his men, but never [tolerates] an infraction of discipline." He is "intrepid to the verge of temerity, though never injudiciously so." Though he displays usually an "unobtrusiveness of demeanour" and an "unaffected modesty," when the times call for action he demonstrates that he possesses a "resolute nature." Though he is "practical enough upon occasion," he betrays sometimes a "certain dreaminess of mood." In all things, that is, Captain Vere avoids exaggerations, extremes. His nickname—Starry Vere—might at first appear ironic to one who, "whatever his sturdy qualities," is "without any brilliant ones." But the stars themselves, unlike the sun, are not flashily brilliant: they are held sturdily fixed in heavenly balance.

Like Melville's admirable maskless men such as Rolfe and Chase, Captain Vere adds to an instinctive wisdom the wisdom of books: he likes unconventional writers, who, free from cant and convention, like Montaigne, honestly, and in the spirit of common sense philosophize upon realities." This love of books, though it deprives him of a certain boisterous "companionable quality" common to his profession, and though it gains him the reputation of possessing a "queer streak of the pedantic," nevertheless underlines the dominant trait of his personality—his utter openness. He is interested in confronting the "realities," which he is so avid to read about, without flinching and without a trace of deception. It is precisely this bluntness (characteristic also of Rolfe and Jack Chase) which, though never cruel, frequently puzzles or startles his colleagues and sets Starry Vere apart. Melville carefully points out that in natures like Captain Vere's, "honesty prescribes to them directness, sometimes far-reaching like that of a migratory fowl that in its flight never heeds when it crosses a frontier."

Captain Vere's crucial action in handling Billy Budd's trial demonstrates that he is the only individual on board the *Indomitable* who understands what White Jacket instinctively learned on his voyage and what Plinlimmon formulated as a philosophy in his pamphlet—the wide and necessary separation of heavenly and earthly wisdom, and the "impossibility" of the application of the one in the province of the other. Captain Vere understands further—and it is this understanding that divides his sympathies and almost unbalances this balanced man—that both kinds of wisdom are right in their place, that the "failure" of one out of its place by no means signifies its insufficiency. It is this insight that enables Captain Vere to sympathize so profoundly with Billy Budd while at the same time arguing so persuasively the necessity of his conviction. At Billy's execution, Captain Vere's emotions, as compelling as the crew's, are simply more intellectually disciplined. As Billy's "God bless Captain Vere" echoes about him, Vere, "either through stoic self-control or a sort of momentary paralysis induced by emotional shock, [stands] erectly rigid as a musket in the ship-armour's rack." When, some time after the Billy Budd incident, Captain Vere lies dying on his ship in the midst of battle, he is heard to murmur "Billy Budd, Billy Budd." A member of Billy's drumhead court is present to testify that the refrain is not whispered with "accents of remorse." On the verge of death, Captain Vere still clearly understands the necessity of his action even as he cries out his affection for his departed sailor.

—James E. Miller, Jr., *A Reader's Guide to Herman Melville*
(New York: Farrar, Straus & Cudahy, 1962), pp. 225–27

Joyce Carol Oates on Melville's Quests and Their Ends

[Joyce Carol Oates (b. 1938) is one of the most distinguished American novelists of her generation and also a prolific critic. She is currently Roger S. Berlind

Distinguished Professor at Princeton University. In this extract, Oates explores the changing view of the quest in Melville's work and his changing philosophy on death as revealed in *Billy Budd*.]

In *Billy Budd*, the quest theme of Melville has run its course. We have no Adamic-turned-Faustian hero, a superman of sorts like Ahab, Pierre, and the confidence-man; we have instead individuals like Billy and Vere and Claggart, one-dimensional, almost passive role-takers in a triangle of archetypal scope.

The problem of *Billy Budd*, then, stems from the disintegration of the quest and from the acceptance of death as not evil—which leads romantically to the sailor's apotheosis in the folklore of his time, and classically to the acceptance of social necessity, of forms and order. But the intent of the work may well transcend this compatible dichotomy to suggest an acceptance of impending death, of annihilation, in somewhat Nirvanic terms, for the work is "angry," or represents part of a "quarrel" only if death is taken, as it conventionally is, to be at least painful and frightening. The terror of the white whale, infinity pressing back upon its perceiver (or creator), becomes here the transcendental dissolving of considerations of good and evil, of struggle, of life itself. Walter Sutton interprets *Billy Budd* in the light of Melville's interest in Buddhism and Schopenhauer, and sees the movement of the novel as a renunciation of the will that is the "highest consummation of life." The Nirvanic quest has no faith in Buddha as a god, but only in Buddhism as an expression of negation. Thus the end of life—by extension, never to have lived—is the equivalent of the Christian's ascension and final communion with his God. So Vere does little to save Billy's life, and Billy's last words—to be contrasted, surely, with the savage rebelliousness of a White Jacket—are words of a positive nature, perhaps of gratitude. The untouched innocence of Billy, his pre-Adamic condition, is saved from the world of experience that wounds Captain Vere; untouched, both are apotheosized and annihilated: "God bless Captain Vere!" Billy says, and his words precede a double death, that of Billy and Vere himself.

The experience of Vere is in broad terms that of the father who manipulates the figure of innocence into the transcendent

Nirvana of nonexperience and nonidentity that he himself will earn, after a time, but that he has reached only after this experience—which invariably wounds—in the painful world of appearances, of good and evil, of constant struggle, and, most perniciously, of unnatural, repressed lusts. For a writer whose aim is to penetrate into a "basic truth," the sustainment of any two points of view will suggest, in the end, the mockery of assigning to one of two antithetical views a positiveness worthy of one's faith—worthy of one's life. The quest ends, ideally, in the negation and not in the compromise or resolution of tension in Melville's irreconcilable world of opposites; it is at once a transcendence and an annihilation, no longer an image of romantic diffusion as in *White Jacket,* surely not an image of the vicious and self-consuming pessimism of *Pierre.*

The intention of this essay has not been to examine critically all facets of Melville's apparent drift into nihilism—this would involve, as well, as close study of Melville's reading of Schopenhauer—but rather to undercut the general tone of simplicity in which Melville is often discussed. The cliché of the "defiant rebel" represents but an arresting of Melville's thought at a point fairly early in his career; a study of Melville's movement away from this stance, as well as to it, is necessary to provide a fair view of the metaphysical and ethical implications of his work. Nineteenth-century in his conception of the forms of fiction and of "characterization," Melville is strikingly contemporary in his conception of the internal tensions that comprise a work. In a sense he is not a writer of "fiction" at all, but a writer of ideas who is using the means of fiction; let us speculate that he used fiction because of its essential ambiguity, its "muteness," and because of the possibility of his hiding behind its disguises. Just as he dares to do no more than hint at the homosexual perversion of sailors in *White Jacket* and *Billy Budd,* so, in mid-nineteenth-century America he can do no more than hint at the blankness behind the age-old negotiable forms of virtue and vice, good and evil, God and the Devil.

—Joyce Carol Oates, "Melville and the Tragedy of Nihilism" (1962), *The Edge of Impossibility: Tragic Forms in Literature* (New York: Vanguard Press, 1972), pp. 81–83

Alan Lebowitz on the Homeward Journey of Benito Cereno

[Alan Lebowitz (b. 1934) is a novelist and professor of English at Tufts University. He is the author of *Progress into Silence: A Study of Melville's Heroes* (1970), from which the following extract is taken. Here, Lebowitz comments on Melville's short tales, in which the focus is no longer on adventures at sea but the homeward journey.]

What is striking about all these short pieces is that Melville's persistent preoccupations, as in the last novels, are those of the wandering seafarer come home. Even in "Benito Cereno" the thrust is curiously landward. The focus is on innocence, not experience. In contrast to the earlier conception of the story, the transfiguring contact with savage terrors is made not by the neophyte-narrator but by the lesser figure of Benito himself, who is not even an American, let alone an Ahab, and whose full story emerges only through his depositions written at a remove from the terrible events. Captain Delano, on the other hand, is a perpetual American innocent. Though at sea, where great adventure is a ready possibility and violent death a central fact of life, the captain of the *Bachelor's Delight* sees and understands no more of the dangers that confront him than the most indifferent and oblivious of Melville's previous bachelors. Yet Melville does not judge him harshly, as he did with similar characters in earlier works. There is in this, perhaps, a curious and moving prescience. Shortly afterward, the Herman Melville who had been to sea with Taji and with Ahab—and had even, like his greatest hero, lived among cannibals—would make a comparable sort of peace with his grim perceptions and his memories. Locked in a dreary job, fixed in a domestic establishment that was clearly deeply troubled, he nonetheless maintained a kind of equilibrium. And however one may regret the loss of energy and passion, there is an integrity to the new role as well as a great private drama.

—Alan Lebowitz, *Progress into Silence: A Study of Melville's Heroes* (Bloomington: Indiana University Press, 1970), pp. 209–10

[Howard Welsh is a former professor of English at the University of Southern Mississippi. In this extract, Welsh examines Melville's idea of race in America as presented in "Benito Cereno."]

In the overall design of the story as a pattern of political implication, I think that what Melville had in mind was something like the following. The slave owner, Aranda, whose chalky skeleton is concealed under the figurehead as an unspoken warning to the remaining Spaniards, having in the first instance adopted the repressive institution of slavery, failed to keep up the repression requisite to the nature of the system. Because he was a generous master and gave the slaves freedom of the deck (he was obviously benighted in somewhat the manner of Delano), the massacre occurred. Aranda's generosity represents Melville's envisioning, at the time the story was written, a voluntary, not war-induced freeing of the slaves by the South. But he saw that the problem would not end with the abolition of the institution, for the continued presence of the blacks when the restraints were gone would be a danger. In the "Supplement" to *Battle-Pieces* Melville spoke of

> . . . the unprecedented position of the Southerners—their position as regards the millions of ignorant manumitted slaves in their midst, for whom some of us now claim the suffrage. . . . In one point of view the coexistence of the two races in the South—whether the negro be bound or free—seems (even as it did to Abraham Lincoln) a grave evil. Emancipation has ridded the country of the reproach, but not wholly of the calamity.

Once he has finally seen the truth, Delano comes to the aid of the Spaniards. After a gory battle the blacks are quelled. Attacking the blacks, even though their savage rebellion occurred in response to their savage mistreatment, seemed natural to Delano; for "who ever heard of a white so far a renegade as to apostatize from his very species almost, by leaguing in against it with negroes?" Delano prevents a general massacre of the blacks in reprisal by the remaining Spaniards, perhaps suggesting that in the South genocide is a near possibility. If that was what Melville had in mind—after the war he would worry that Northern rigor against the South, the "misrule after strife" he speaks of in *Clarel,* might provoke "exterminating hatred of race toward race"—he could cite good authority. Jefferson had spoken of the "deep rooted prejudices entertained by the whites," the "ten thousand recollections, by the blacks, of the injuries they have sustained," "distinctions which nature has made; and many other convulsions, which will probably never end but in the extermination of our or of the other race." In any event, a civilization is done for; and it is represented by Cereno. The bloody uprising of the blacks, however, merely hastens the working of a decadence long since begun, of which Aranda's indulgence of the slaves was but a terminal symptom. Not long before Cereno's death, Delano insists to Cereno, ". . . you are saved: what has cast such a shadow upon you?" Cereno's answer is not the expected "Babo," but rather "The negro."

—Howard Welsh, "The Politics of Race in 'Benito Cereno,'"
American Literature 46, No. 4 (January 1975): 563–64

KERMIT VANDERBILT ON THE STRUCTURE AND CHARACTERS OF "BENITO CERENO"

[Kermit Vanderbilt, formerly a professor of American literature at San Diego State University, is the author of *Charles Eliot Norton: Apostle of Culture in a Democracy* (1959) and *The Achievement of William Dean Howells* (1968). In this extract, Vanderbilt examines the structure of "Benito Cereno" and the characters of Cereno and Delano.]

Melville conceived "Benito Cereno" in two forward-moving actions, a deputation resumé by Cereno, a brief flashback, and a concluding epilogue. Transparent in outline and, for Melville, remarkably matter-of-fact in style, the tale harbors numerous masks, disguises, and allusive cross-identities, so that a reader's slowly developing sense is of a coiled and knotted inquiry into the slaveship mutiny and the vengeful aftermath. The story opens upon a "gray" dawn, "mute and calm," pointedly ushering in the ominous mood and prevailing theme of the story. In blatantly ironic counterpoint, Melville introduces the American Captain Delano "of a singularly good nature" who reluctantly, if ever, is given "to indulge in personal alarms, any way involving the imputation of malign evil in man." Delano boards Cereno's battered Spanish ship and, during his day-long suspicions, never pierces to the reality that he is the guest at a masked black slave insurrection. Critics of the story have written far too much on the pointed irony of Delano's innocent puzzlements and moral clichés. In the process, such criticism has failed to distinguish between a reader's immediate, and largely shared, experience of Delano's quandary as opposed to one's later understanding of it. Coming to the story as a first-time reader, one will discover Melville's using Delano for two purposes more important than injecting an Emersonian naïveté which one may wish to scoff at in retrospect. First, Delano establishes for the reader the plausible, orthodox view that slavery is a two-way institution that separates men into unyielding masters and dog-like servants. Through Delano's perplexed consciousness, Cereno becomes the felt oppressor. I shall grant that the extent of this response will vary with a reader's quickness to realize some possibility of the black mutiny. Delano speculates on what *kind* of master of this strange foreign slaveship Cereno is. But he never doubts that Cereno is, as black "servant" Babo insistently addresses him, the "master." Or when the imposing black Atufal appears on deck, in chains for the past sixty days because, we are told, he had given Cereno "peculiar cause of offense," the reader recognizes, with Delano, the historical validity of such petty intimidation of master upon slave. Or in a parallel scene, after shaving Cereno, Babo appears on deck, his cheek bleeding from a razor wound inflicted apparently by Cereno because the slave "had given master one little scratch."

Whatever gain the reader has made beyond the perceptions of Delano this late in the day, he can still assent in his own way to Delano's human conclusion: "Ah, this slavery breeds ugly passions in man." And again later, we feel the same truth that Norton had observed, that even the most lenient of plantation gentlemen suffered their own debilitating penalty as slave masters. Delano one last time before departing urges leniency for

Atufal and adds, "Ah, Don Benito, for all the license you permit in some things, I fear lest, at bottom, you are a bitter hard master." When Delano believes that Cereno "shrank; and this time . . . from a genuine twinge of conscience," we feel that Delano very well may be observing accurately, may have genuinely awakened Cereno's conscience at last to what it means to be a master—or a slave.

At the same time that he grants the reader a series of orthodox responses to bondage and oppressive mastery, Delano serves a second and more vital function. During his long day of private and open questionings, he creates a webwork of ambiguous facts which Melville can fully exploit in Cereno's deposition for the Lima court. As we shall see, the ultimate effect of Melville's unfolding drama of slavery at that later stage of the tale goes well beyond ironic qualification or reversal of Delano's mistaken conclusions. Instead, we become aware of the intricate complicity of all the actors in the story. To this end, the crucial moments observed by Delano on the opening day are those which suggest or prefigure the merging roles and identities of masters and slaves. Added to those I have already cited, such moments include Delano's fancied observation before boarding Cereno's *San Dominick,* that the ship is like a holy retreat and the blacks like "Black Friars" strolling within the cloisters. (I shall later treat Melville's various allusions to the Church.) Delano soon observes the stern-piece with its central carving of "a dark satyr in a mask, holding his foot on the prostrate neck of a writhing figure, likewise masked."

In addition to these mutually masked oppressor-and-oppressed figures, the ship carries below its canvased bow the words "*Seguid vuestro jefe,*" an injunction to which multiple meanings will accrue. Cereno appears to Delano "like some hypochondriac abbot" and black Babo's "offices" to his "master" seem "filial or fraternal," though appropriate for a "pleasing body-servant . . . whom a master need be on no stiffly superior terms with, but may treat with familiar trust; less a servant than a devoted companion." When Cereno momentarily withdraws from his conversation with Delano, Babo "encircle[s] his master"; Babo appears "a sort of privy-counselor" to his master; or they seem, face to face, to have "the air of conspirators." Delano goes so far as to question if Cereno might in some manner be "in complicity with the blacks," but reassures himself that "they were too stupid." After Babo appears on deck with a cheek bleeding, having previously nicked Cereno during the shaving scene, Delano is relieved to see master and servant reappear closely paired: "But a sort of love-quarrel, after all, thought Captain Delano." The revealing hint here, not unusual in Melville, is that the antagonists have attained a homoerotic closeness.

—Kermit Vanderbilt, " 'Benito Cereno': Melville's Fable of Black Complicity," *Southern Review* 12, No. 2 (April 1976): 314–16

EDWARD H. ROSENBERRY ON HISTORY IN *BILLY BUDD*

[Edward H. Rosenberry, formerly a professor of English at the University of Delaware, is the author of *Melville and the Comic Spirit* (1955) and *Melville* (1979), from which the following extract is taken. Here, Rosenberry explores the historical backdrop against which the moral story of *Billy Budd* is set.]

A new phase of creation had clearly been entered when Billy took fresh shape as a spiritual innocent, more sinned against than sinning. As his moral profile clarified, a vacuum developed around the need for an evil principle in the story, and John Claggart, Master-at-arms, was born, at first in outline, then fuller and fuller in detail as Melville pursued the mystery of his malice and duplicity. The clearing of Billy's guilt as a mutineer, the placing of a false accusation in the mouth of Claggart, and the transformation of Billy's crime to murder are easy steps in the logic of the creative imagination. All that remains to the essential framework of the great parable in the making is the judge, the all-powerful authority to whose lot it falls to pronounce upon the moral character of the acts he has witnessed and upon the fate of the transgressor. Only at this stage, evidently, when the conception of the troubled captain had added a third dimension to his developing drama, did Melville begin to flesh out a historical scene, to paint the stage of time and place on which his tragic collision of moral forces could achieve human credibility. It is at this point, finally, that *Billy Budd* takes on its semi-polished character as historical romance, a tale of the Revolutionary summer of 1797.

In constructing this quasi-factual backdrop of events Melville strove for two kinds of credibility. In the most general sense he was concerned, as he had always been, that his story not be dismissed as a 'monstrous fable,' the fate he had feared for *Moby-Dick,* but that it be accepted as 'a narration essentially having less to do with fable than with fact' (ch. 28). What he meant by 'fact,' as he explains in the next sentence, was 'Truth uncompromisingly told'—a definition which, in broadening rather than narrowing the field of reference, left him as much freedom for romance as if he had chosen the term 'fable.' What he wished to avoid, he wrote in chapter 11, was mere plot juggling or manipulation of events for some preconceived outcome, such as contriving a prior relationship between hero and villain in order to rationalize the enmity that moves them toward catastrophe. What he sought was a romance compounded of the sort of 'mysteriousness' with which the very reality of life is charged: in this instance, a drama rooted not in mechanical causes but in the profound enigmas at the bottom of such natures as those of his three 'phenomenal' principals.

What history, or a show of history, gave him was not documented certainties of the past, but verisimilitude and motivation. For these purposes he did as much research as he had to and no more. His principal sources were William James's *Naval History of Great Britain* and Robert Southey's *Life of Nelson,* and most of what is specific and authoritative from those sources he worked into chapters 3 to 5. His first object was to establish an atmosphere in which the moral crisis of his story could grow. This atmosphere was admirably supplied by the tensions resulting from, on the one hand, the grave blow to British naval morale in the unprecedented mutinies of Spithead and the Nore in the spring of 1797, and on the other hand, Britain's crucial need of her sea power as a last line of defense against the rising power of France and Spain in the succeeding months and years, culminating in Trafalgar. He located his action on a 74-gun ship-of-the-line with the British fleet in the Mediterranean; he made use of contemporaneous evils such as impressment and the enlistment of criminals, as well as the disciplinary trauma of threatened mutiny; and he seized on the shortage of scouting frigates of which Nelson complained in that campaign to explain the detached service which was to force Captain Vere into the isolated role of judge and executioner. In addition to these solid historical aids, he used the character of Nelson himself as a touchstone of naval heroism, establishing as his primary virtue an impassioned sense of duty.

At some point in the developing conception of his plot, though not at first as was once generally believed, Melville recalled and adapted to his purposes another chapter of naval history, the notorious execution in 1842 of three suspected mutineers on the United States brig *Somers* by order of the captain, Alexander Slidell Mackenzie. The deeply moot question of the captain's authority and procedure was impressed on the American public at large by the fact that a young midshipman among the victims of Mackenzie's summary justice, though less virtuous than the legendary 'Handsome Sailor,' was the son of the Secretary of War; and it was impressed on Melville in particular by the fact that the first lieutenant, whose advice and consent was demanded by the captain, was Melville's cousin, Guert Gansevoort. The trial scene (ch. 21), at the conclusion of which Melville explicitly cites the *Somers* case as an analogue, is shot through with echoes of a story which he had known and pondered for nearly half a century. Even Billy's famous last words, 'God bless Captain Vere,' reflect those of one of the *Somers* men, who cried, 'God bless the flag.'

—Edward H. Rosenberry, *Melville* (London: Routledge & Kegan Paul, 1979), pp. 110–12

ELIZABETH HARDWICK ON BARTLEBY'S MADDENING SILENCE

[Elizabeth Hardwick (b. 1916) is a professor of English at Barnard College as well as a prominent critic and novelist. Among her collections of essays are *A View of My Own* (1962) and *Bartleby in Manhattan* (1983). In

Out of some sixteen thousand words, Bartleby, the cadaverous and yet blazing center of all our attention, speaks only thirty-seven short lines, more than a third of which are a repetition of a single line, the celebrated, the "famous," I think one might call it, retort: *I would prefer not to.* No, "retort" will not do, representing as it does too great a degree of active mutuality for Bartleby—*reply* perhaps.

Bartleby's reduction of language is of an expressiveness literally limitless. Few characters in fiction, if indeed any exist, have been able to say all they wish in so striking, so nearly speechless a manner. The work is, of course, a sort of fable of inanition, and returning to it, as I did, mindful of the old stone historical downtown and the new, insatiable necropolis of steel and glass, lying on the vegetation of the participial *declining* this and that, I found it possible to wish that "Bartleby, the Scrivener" was just itself, a masterpiece without the challenge of its setting, Wall Street. Still, the setting does not flee the mind, even if it does not quite bind itself either, the way unloaded furniture seems immediately bound to its doors and floors.

Melville has written his story in a cheerful, confident, rather optimistic, Dickensian manner. Or at least that is the manner in which it begins. In the law office, for instance, the copyists and errand-boy are introduced with their Dickensian *tics* and their tic-names: Nippers, Turkey, and Ginger Nut. An atmosphere of comedy, of small, amusing, busy particulars, surrounds Bartleby and his large, unofficial (not suited to an office) articulations, which are nevertheless clerkly and even, perhaps, clerical.

The narrator, a mild man of the law with a mild Wall Street business, is a "rather elderly man," as he says of himself at the time of putting down his remembrances of Bartleby. On the edge of retirement, the lawyer begins to think about that "singular set of men," the law-copyists or scriveners he has known in his thirty years of practice. He notes that he has seen nothing of these men in print and, were it not for the dominating memory of Bartleby, he might have told lighthearted professional anecdotes, something perhaps like the anecdotes of servants come and gone, such as we find in the letters of Jane Carlyle, girls from the country who are not always unlike the Turkeys, Nippers, and Ginger Nuts.

The lawyer understands that no biography of Bartleby is possible because "no materials exist," and indeed the work is not a character sketch and not a section of a "life," even though it ends in death. Yet the device of memory is not quite the way it works out, because each of Bartleby's thirty-seven lines, with their riveting variations, so slight as to be almost painful to the mind taking note of them, must be produced at the right pace and accompanied by the requests that occasion them. At a certain point, Bartleby must "gently disappear behind the screen," which, in a way, is a present rather than a past. In the end, Melville's structure is magical because the lawyer creates Bartleby by *allowing* him to be, a decision of nicely unprofessional impracticality. The competent, but scarcely strenuous, office allows Bartleby, although truly the allowance arises out of the fact that the lawyer is a far better man than he knows himself to be. And he is taken by surprise to learn of his tireless curiosity about the incurious ghost, Bartleby.

—Elizabeth Hardwick, "Bartleby in Manhattan" (1981), *Bartleby in Manhattan and Other Essays* (New York: Random House, 1983), pp. 218–20

JOYCE SPERER ADLER ON MELVILLE'S ATTITUDE TOWARD WAR IN *BILLY BUDD*

[Joyce Sperer Adler (b. 1915) is the author of *Attitudes toward "Race" in Guyanese Literature* (1967), *Language and Man* (1970), and *War in Melville's Imagination* (1981), from which the following extract is taken. Here, Adler argues that Melville uses *Billy Budd* to express his horror of war and the "war machine."]

Billy Budd, Sailor concentrates Melville's philosophy of war and lifts it to its highest point of development. Its themes are recapitulations and extensions of those he had many times developed, and its poetic conceptions are the offspring of earlier ones that had embodied his ideas concerning the "greatest of evils." Even the manuscript record of his revision gives evidence of his need to express as perfectly as possible his thinking about the ill that had been at the center of his imagination for almost half a century and his vision of the "civilized" and "Christian" world in which the essence of war and evil is one. His reluctance to finish is understandable. In his seventies he could not count on another chance to set forth so scrupulously his view of the man-of-war world as a parody of the Christianity it feigns or to awaken other imaginations to "holier" values than those civilized man had lived by.

The view of *Billy Budd* as the final stage in the development of Melville's philosophy of war embraces both the work's abhorrence of war and the war machine (the feeling ignored by those who, in the classical argument about *Billy Budd,* see it as a "testament of acceptance") and its genuinely affirmative, non-ironic, and luminous aspects (the qualities set aside by those who see it in its totality as irony, rejection, or darkness alone). Along with Melville's continued rejection of the world of war there is in *Billy Budd* a new affirmation that within that world's most cruel contradictions lies the potentiality of its metamorphosis.

It is now generally believed that *Billy Budd, Sailor* was originally intended for inclusion in *John Marr and Other Sailors* since an early draft of the ballad with which the story ends goes back to 1886 when other poems with short prose introductions in the collection were being composed. But as one can see from the Hayford and Sealts genetic text, which traces the changes Melville made during the years of *Billy Budd*'s composition, Melville sensed early the potentialities that a development of the basic situation—the execution of a sailor in wartime—could have. It could present an unforgettable picture of the essential nature of the world of war and, at the same time, suggest its complexities, which the imagination of man must penetrate. The revisions move steadily in the direction of realizing these potentialities ever more fully, until in the end *Billy Budd* becomes a work to remain in the reader's memory as simultaneously one of the most simple of fictional works—in terms of story—and one of the most complex in terms of what is implied by the art with which the story is presented.

By the time of his last work Melville was so experienced a poet and narrator that he could rely solely on poetic conceptions integrated into narrative to carry his ideas. For this reason it is possible to consider all main aspects of the work in the course of recalling the story.

What happens in *Billy Budd,* with the exception of what takes place within the psyche of the crew, is what Melville had all along demonstrated must necessarily happen—what is, in that sense, fated—in the "present civilisation of the world." Impressed from the English merchant ship *Rights-of-Man* to serve the king on the battleship *Bellipotent* in 1797, the year of the Great Mutiny during the Napoleonic wars, Billy is almost literally *White-Jacket's* sailor "shorn of all rights." Young and of considerable physical and personal beauty, like Melville's typical "Handsome Sailor" in aspect though not like him a "spokesman," called "peacemaker" and "jewel" by the merchantman's captain, and "flower of the flock" and a "beauty" by the lieutenant who carries him off, he is from the first the symbol of the good and beauty "out of keeping" and doomed in the world of war. He is, at the same time, representative of sailors as a class, as the title *Billy Budd, Sailor* conveys. The words of John Marr, describing seamen generally, apply to him: "Taking things as fated merely,/Child-like through the world ye spanned;/Nor holding unto life too dearly,/ . . . Barbarians of man's simpler nature,/Unworldly servers of the world." He is shortly seen to represent also the jewel and flower of youth sacrificed to war, like the soldiers in *Battle-Pieces* "nipped like blossoms," willing children sent through fire as sacrifices to a false god, fated to die because an older generation has failed to rectify wrongs that lead to war. In either aspect—representative or outstanding—he incorporates *White-Jacket's* conception of a sailor as the "image of his Creator."
　　　　—Joyce Sperer Adler, *War in Melville's Imagination* (New York: New York University Press, 1981), pp. 160–61

WILLIAM D. RICHARDSON ON THE CONFLICT BETWEEN
CIVILIZATION AND BARBARISM IN "BENITO CERENO"

[William D. Richardson is the author of *Melville's
"Benito Cereno": An Interpretation with Annotated
Text and Concordance* (1987), from which the following extract is taken. Here, Richardson believes that
Melville's central theme in "Benito Cereno" is the clash
between civilization and barbarism and that this theme
is treated on two levels.]

Melville's "Benito Cereno," a tale of a shipboard slave rebellion, has an obvious political theme: the clash between modern
civilization and barbarism. Within the context of this theme,
Melville addresses some of the most fundamental political
problems confronting man—problems involving the tensions
between conventional and natural inequality; between the
preservation of existing political orders and revolution;
between the demands of a secular state and those of a state
captivated by religion; between democracy and aristocracy;
between the requirements of justice and those of the law; and,
finally, between the dictates of reason and those of unreason-
ing forces such as prejudice—particularly racial prejudice.

The subtle way in which Melville treats the civilization-
barbarism theme may explain why many reviewers of "Benito
Cereno" fail to perceive either the number and complexity of
the political problems addressed in the work or Melville's
teachings about them. In addressing these problems, particularly that of racial prejudice, Melville approaches them on two
different levels. On the surface of the work, he seems to be
speaking to the ordinary citizen of America—the white,
Northern or Southern man of commerce who is the product of
modern political philosophy's overwhelming sway in America.
This citizen reader of "Benito Cereno" derives a simple meaning from the tale: slave uprisings are unquestionably wrong
and their participants, accordingly, inevitably must succumb to
such superior white men of commerce as Captain Amasa
Delano. In this view, Delano is the tale's hero; he embodies
those qualities which the average American citizen admires:
hard work, Protestantism, bravery, loyalty, honesty, frugality,

and a sense of justice. This citizen perspective of "Benito Cereno" largely explains why the tale consistently evoked such encomiums as "thrilling" and "powerful" from reviewers who were themselves average citizens addressing like audiences.

However, the very art for which Melville is praised (writing a good short story) is also responsibile for veiling another meaning of the tale—one which is sympathetic to portions of what I will term the "citizen perspective," but antipathetic to much of it. This other, deeper meaning reveals itself only through the most painstaking attention to Melville's use of symbolism, contradiction, and structure. It is veiled partly because its teaching does not support the citizen perspective addressed on the tale's surface and, for that reason, it could be dangerous to and subversive of the American regime. Another reason the deeper meaning remains veiled is related to but nonetheless separate from the first: Melville seeks to address and teach those individuals who possess the capacity of mind to unravel the hidden meaning, a dedication to the pursuit of truth, and the strength of character requisite to a proper understanding and use of the veiled teaching. It would appear that those to whom this knowledge would be most appropriate would be either statesmen or the teachers of statesmen. Consequently, this hidden meaning hereafter will be referred to as the "statesman perspective." Before one can attempt to understand this statesman perspective, however, it is necessary that one comprehend the simple or citizen perspective as fully as possible. The surmounting of this preliminary obstacle is facilitated by an understanding of the political environment of the 1850s. ⟨. . .⟩

To understand both the way in which Melville attempts to present his teaching in these volatile times as well as that teaching itself, it is necessary to be meticulous in one's reading of "Benito Cereno." This effort is enhanced, to a considerable extent, by the knowledge that the tale is woven around a published account of an actual event which occurred in 1805. The initial entrance into the mysteries of "Benito Cereno," therefore, lies outside its text in part of a work by the real-life Captain Amasa Delano entitled *A Narrative of Voyages and Travels*. On their surfaces, Delano's autobiographical account and Melville's "Benito Cereno" seem very similar. For example, both versions have narrative sections which are bolstered by depositions from courts of law, some of the names in both tales are identical, and the main story-lines are very similar. These similarities, however, in no way detract either from Melville's stature as an author and teacher or from the greatness of "Benito Cereno." Melville obviously came upon Delano's account and was intrigued by what it said (and could be made to say) about man. The real-life Delano, the hero of his own tale and a main character in Melville's, certainly appears to have been blind to the lessons Melville saw in the autobiographical account. For Melville, the real-life incident contained the necessary ingredients to reveal man more starkly than any purely fictional account ever could.

> —William D. Richardson, "Interpretive Essay," *Melville's "Benito Cereno": An Interpretation with Annotated Text and Concordance* (Durham, NC: Carolina Academic Press, 1987), pp. 69–71

PETER A. SMITH ON BARTLEBY'S DUAL ENTROPY

[Peter A. Smith is a professor of English at Wesleyan University. In this extract, Smith explores the informational and physical entropy of Bartleby's existence in the Dead Letter Office.]

In "Bartleby the Scrivener" we see the effects of both informational entropy and physical entropy on the title character. Bartleby's determination to keep his isolation intact is the result of his daily witnessing of the effects of entropy on information exchange prior to his employment as a scrivener. As the narrator informs us, "one little item of rumor" about Bartleby's past had reached him: Bartleby had once been a clerk in the Dead Letter Office at Washington. The narrator's relaying of the rumor despite his acknowledgement that the tale seems to reach a natural conclusion at the point of Bartleby's death ("there would seem to be little need for proceeding further in this history") indicates how vital he feels this "item" has been to his understanding of Bartleby.

As a clerk in the Dead Letter Office, Bartleby had aided the entropic process in its obstruction of human communication. The burning of the "dead" letters is a worst-case example of informational entropy. The law of entropy, as it applies to information theory, states that entropy can only increase during the process of transmitting a message from sender to receiver; it can never decrease. Information can be lost during transmission, but it can never be gained. At the Dead Letter Office lay thousands of examples of the complete futility of attempting to communicate; here entropy not only distorts and disrupts, but completely destroys communication: "On errands of life, these letters speed to death."

The lesson that Bartleby carries with him out of the Dead Letter Office and into the Master in Chancery's office is that there is no point in attempting to exchange information through conventional means. If anything, Bartleby's "new" occupation as a scrivener only serves to reinforce what he had learned from his "old" occupation as dead letter clerk. As a scrivener, Bartleby only copies documents—he does no creative or meaningful writing. And the documents that he is called upon to reproduce merely help to perpetuate a futile legal system: the Chancery system was notorious for keeping cases tied up in courts for years. All of the documents that Bartleby must copy are nothing more than parodies of attempts to exchange information, as useless to those who need help as are letters which never reach their destinations.

It is significant that most of Bartleby's refusals to do anything other than copy involve the Master in Chancery's requests that Bartleby proofread one of these documents with another person. For Bartleby, to aid in reciting these useless documents would be to take part in a painful parody of human communication. Bartleby realizes that this proofreading with others is a sham because it involves "going through the motions" of exchanging information, when actually the words being read and spoken are merely form without content. At least burning letters had been, for Bartleby, an honest admission that the whole transaction is pointless—it involved no charade.

—Peter A. Smith, "Entropy in Melville's 'Bartleby the Scrivener,'" *Centennial Review* 32, No. 2 (Spring 1988): 156–58

WILLIAM H. HILDEBRAND ON BARTLEBY'S ISOLATION

[William H. Hildebrand is a professor of English at Kent State University and the author of *A Study of* Alastor (1954). In this extract, Hildebrand argues that Melville's quest for independence from Christian morality gave rise to Bartleby's isolation in a sterile and godless world.]

In a very urgent sense, the entire story exists for the sake of the naked room, with Bartleby at its forlorn center. There the lawyer reenacts the sin of Cain by not loving enough and so, at the end, abides in death, entombed in a world that is the Dead Letter Office writ large—where the "letter" of rationalism "killeth" faith, hope, and charity; where no "spirit giveth life" (II Cor. 3.6). And his description of this "diabolical" act as the tearing or breaking of the human bond suggests that in his fall we can discern, as in a glass darkly, the anterior moment of fault represented by Bartleby—fratricide following necessarily from the breaking of the bond with God.

On the analogy of the Genesis sequence of fall and fratricide, then, and taking his innately disordered soul as original sin, we can speculate that Bartleby's fault involves the dynamics of temptation and fall, of freedom and knowledge—a breaking of the bond with God that leads to mortality, estrangement, exile; to an abiding in death. Bartleby's fallenness, as revealed in his gloom, forlornness, spiritual and physical inappetence, and negative preferences, intimates the prior use of freedom to violate the creative limits of an ontological relationship on which the vital order of being depended. The result is the disorder of meaninglessness, the "sheer vacancy" of non-being following the loss of the ontological ground, a diminution of and aversion to life, a gloomy knowledge, and a freedom that can only prefer not to, can only build desolate places. This is the freedom-from of self-autonomy, of "mere self-interest," which distrustfully regards all bonds, whether with God or fellow beings, as confinement and feels them as bondage. The constituents of Bartleby's gloom—solitude, sadness, exile, emptiness, death—reflect the primal fault and symbolize the absence of God, which echoes as "sheer vacancy" throughout the walled world of the story. Thus the evil that rises in the

empty room is the stinging knowledge of "penal hopelessness," for the temptation to despair and the knowledge of
emptiness, absence, meaninglessness, are experientially one,
though reflection can analyze them into moments. And
Bartleby's fault incestuously breeds the sin of not loving the
brother that is spiritual death; meridionally, *acedia,* the aversion
to God and the opposite of *caritas,* leads to hopelessness and
death. Thus Bartleby's numb detachment from everything is
like a referred pain in medicine—a self-absorption registering
the greater malady of self-idolatry, of pride, as evidenced in his
"wilfulness," "haughtiness," "calm disdain," and "perverse-
ness." This suggests that the breaking of the ontological bond
leads to self-bondage and that the gloomy abyss where his
soul repines is in the self. This is the ultimate development of
what, following Augustine, Pascal calls concupiscence and
Ricoeur the "evil infinite of human desire"—desire licensed by
the rejection of human finiteness and self-entranced by the limitless freedom to desire infinitely—as Ricoeur says, desire "taking possession of knowing, of willing, of doing, and of being . . ."

Melville himself had been swept up in that romance of self
and desire called the romantic sublime—the human spirit's
declaration of independence from the laws of time and space.
In the giddy exhilaration of exploring the demonic wastes
of titanic self-assertion with Ahab, he had trumpeted to
Hawthorne the "NO! in thunder" of "self-sovereignty," pro-
claiming that those who say "yes, lie; and all men who say no"
travel light, crossing "the frontiers into Eternity with nothing . . . but the Ego." But in Bartleby freedom has shriveled into
the sullen I-prefer-not-to of hopelessness, and self-sovereignty
has turned to dead-walls. This is the meaning of his characteristic attitude: motionless in reverie before a viewless, dead-
wall window, with only a small ray of light falling from "far
above . . . as from a very small opening in a dome"; or asleep
in death against "the dead-wall," curled fetus-like on the "soft
imprisoned turf."

Of Melville a few years after "Bartleby," Hawthorne observed
that he could "neither believe nor be comfortable in his unbelief." "Bartleby" testifies to the precision of Hawthorne's perception. Melville's anguished dialectical suspension over the

abyss—the symbol of God's transcendence experienced as estrangement—is reflected in the story's radical ambiguity, in the strained relations between its narrative and its metaphorical senses. For in "Bartleby" the metaphorical sense not only refines, amplifies, and ornaments; it often runs counter to, opposes, the narrative syntax. In effect, the lawyer and Bartleby sink inexorably from walled-in chambers through ever deeper glooms to the Tombs of Justice and the Dead Letter Office; even the moments of high drollery are witnesses of absurdity; and the lawyer's valedictory sigh, "Ah, Bartleby! Ah humanity!", voices the hopelessness of life in a world without underlying meaning, purpose, or value. But that is not the whole story.

"Bartleby" is not finally a "cadaverous triumph," a counsel of despair, a brief for nihilism, or even an assertion of scepticism. Through the cross-weavings of the figural design, the metaphorical sense, though dimmed by tragic hues, affirms the primary human values of love over hate, hope over despair, life over death. It affirms them indirectly, to be sure, but that is the way of tragedy. And it affirms them Biblically, too, in the central struggle between brotherly love and resentment, as well as in certain small, radiant symbols of the presence of a mystery transcending that of evil. The dome light and the soft imprisoned turf, with its intimations of Eden persisting "by some strange magic" of antenatal nostalgia in the "heart of the eternal pyramids," represents the broken relationship potentially recollected in the "new commandment," by which "sons of Adam" may become "sons of God." The lawyer's failure to love, figurally related to Bartleby's prior fault, is tragic, of course, but not meaningless. It brings the lucidity of suffering— at the end he, like Bartleby, knows where he is, knows that he abides in death. Their despair, then, is not the worst kind, for it knows itself as despair, knows that the very stuff of despair is estrangement from God.

The central emptiness in the story, then, is not the nothingness of Nietzsche but the vanity and idolatry of the Old Testament prophets to whom nothingness was radical but contingent evil; and the absence of God is not the non-existence of atheism but the God-forsakenness of unbelief. For the misery of "Bartleby" is rooted in a terrible loss of God and utter despair of humanity. By fashioning a story that becomes a metaphor of the locus of fault—the empty room—Melville discloses referentially that the penal solitudes where the human soul languishes are in the abyss of self. Thus the word forlorn, chiming somberly throughout the story, works as it does in "Ode to a Nightingale," tolling us back sadly to the "sole self."

In "Bartleby" Melville "strikes the uneven balance" by means of the "black conceit." He weighs the modern world by representing life apart from God according to the traditional Christian understanding of individual and corporate human guilt and responsibility for evil and sin.

—William H. Hildebrand, " 'Bartleby' and the Black Conceit," *Studies in Romanticism* 27, No. 2 (Summer 1988): 310–13

JOHN SAMSON ON TRUTH AND FICTION IN *BILLY BUDD*

[John Samson (b. 1953) is a professor of English at Texas Tech University and the author of *White Lies: Melville's Narratives of Facts* (1989), from which the following extract is taken. Here, Samson maintains that the character of Billy Budd remains enigmatic because fictional narration and the realities of human experience are unbridgeable.]

Melville gives his last, unfinished work the parenthetical subtitle (*An inside narrative*), indicating that *Billy Budd, Sailor* is vitally concerned with what goes on inside the narrative process and that narrative itself is concerned with the attempt to get inside events, here to find the inner truth about the title character. But the relation between title and subtitle is one of contrast, for all the considerable narrative tactics employed by the novel's characters (who are in a sense narrators along with the book's narrator)—the historical analogues, the biographical memories, the Christian patterns, the nautical legends—all fail to get the inside story of Billy. But for that part of the title that describes his work—"*Sailor*"—Billy remains an enigma, the narrative remains another white lie. The distance between the facts of human experience and the truthful narration of that experience remains unbridgeable. Moreover, as Stanton Garner has convincingly demonstrated, the facts themselves here are more than questionable, they are wrong; and intentionally so. The central issue in *Billy Budd,* that is to say, is the inability of narrative to explain natural phenomena, the inapplicability of past historical patterns to account for present occurrences, and the crucial fictionality of "factual" narrative.

Before the narrative itself Melville places a dedication to Jack Chase that further indicates this problematization. To transfer Jack from *White-Jacket's* fictional *Neversink* to the historical *United States*—in essence inverting the creative process Melville had followed in his narratives—breaks down the distinction between fact and fiction and may also be a sly joke at the expense of those who have read his novels as autobiographies. And to dedicate *Billy Budd* to that ridiculous spinner of ahistorical and self-serving yarns signals an extraordinary level of irony, directed, I believe, back toward his previous narratives of facts. Like Jack, Melville's narratives of facts have been consistently misread as considerably lighter, more positive than they indeed are, an issue of much concern to critics who see *Billy Budd* as Melville's final "testament of faith." Thus Jack Chase signifies that other J. C. whose historicity—like that of Billy, who is frequently identified as a Christ-figure—is so much at issue in the late nineteenth century, and again crucial to the issue is a contrast between historical or natural fact and the faith or confidence one can have in narratives to represent those facts. In *White-Jacket* Jack Chase's station high in the elitist main-top places him in sharp contrast to Melville's ocean, in which Melville immerses his narrator to little effect and indicates another facet of the facts/narrative opposition. Nature and an understanding of it that is essentially spiritual—albeit dangerous, as Pip's immersion shows—are opposed by a false and essentially politicized faith in narrative. Nature, what is outside man and his institutions, opposes what is inside narrative—its ideology, its tropology, what Hayden White calls *The Content of the Form.* Melville's presentation of these issues in *Billy Budd,* of concern to Melville throughout his earlier narratives of facts and particularly powerful in *Moby-Dick,* shows this final work to be a metanarrative conclusion to his examination of his culture's white lies.

—John Samson, *White Lies: Melville's Narratives of Facts* (Ithaca, NY: Cornell University Press, 1989), pp. 211–13

SUSAN WEINER ON THE USE OF LEGAL DOCUMENTS IN "BENITO CERENO"

[Susan Weiner (b. 1946) is the author of *Law in Art: Melville's Major Fiction and Nineteenth-Century American Law* (1992). In this extract, Weiner explores the use of legal documents and historical records in "Benito Cereno," arguing that Melville's selection of documents reflects mid–nineteenth-century attempts to justify slavery.]

Melville's manner of adapting his source indicates that he was interested in how selective facts and their inclusion in an official form determine human experience. Melville extracts much of the basis for the fictional portion of his story from the legal documents of his source, then creates fictional documents based on historical accounts to substantiate his own narrative. Thus he uses issues concerning law as a basis for fiction while giving fiction the illusion of fact through legal documentation. The restoration of the historical source magnifies this distortion and intensifies the manipulated quality of both fiction and law that further undermines our confidence in either. The accentuation of the manipulated character of so-called objective legal documents makes the results brought about by legal judgments appear unjust.

Melville also seems to have accentuated the problems of legal form which he found in his source material. He includes and extends the difficulties that the historical Delano merely glossed over. Melville's narrator introduces his documentary record with a statement similar to Delano's version. The fictional statement also reflects the discrepancy between the "officialness" of the documents and their inherent contradictions. Thus the narrator explains: "The following extracts, translated from one of the official Spanish documents, will it is hoped, shed light on the preceding narrative, as well as, in the first place, reveal the true port of departure and true history of the *San Dominick's* voyage." Although citing its official status, the narrator undercuts the document with his qualified language as well as his selection of only one of several possible documents. He further subverts the validity of the deposition by identifying it as a partial translation of one witness who may or may not have been mentally unstable. Benito Cereno's testimony is accepted only because other witnesses corroborated it rather than because it offered direct evidence.

The legal documents Melville creates increase the problems of those presented in his source. Like the historical documents, the fictional documents are provided as an explanation of mysterious and troubling events: "If the Deposition have served as the key to fit into the lock of the complications which precede it, then, as a vault whose door has been flung back, the *San Dominick's* hull lies open today." But this is qualified by the fact that the documents are presented in such a way as to raise doubts about their validity. The narrator consistently intervenes with commentary, calling attention to lists which are omitted, documents which are unspecified, and recollections of which only portions are offered. Events are selectively reported and selectively suppressed, and the reader does not know what material would have been relevant to events had it been included. The reader then becomes even more uncertain as to the significance of the material that is provided. In a rather heavy-handed way, the narrator obliquely refers to large blocks of material that he will not tell us about. Yet he does supply what is needed to convict the rebel slaves:

> The deposition then proceeds with recapitulatory remarks, and a partial renumeration of the negroes, making record of their individual part in the past events, with a view to furnishing, according to command of the court, the data whereon to found the criminal sentences to be pronounced.

The documents are created to supply the official grounds for the preconceived verdict, thereby reflecting mid-nineteenth-century society which used the law to reinforce the already established fact of slavery.

—Susan Weiner, " 'Benito Cereno' and the Failure of Law," *Arizona Quarterly* 47, No. 2 (Summer 1991): 20–22

JOHN HAEGERT ON "BENITO CERENO" AS DETECTIVE FICTION

[John Haegert is a professor of English at the University of Evansville. In this extract, Haegert argues that Melville's literary techniques (especially his use of melodrama) in "Benito Cereno" are similar to those used in detective fiction.]

Melville's reliance on melodrama in constructing *Benito Cereno* is closely allied to his use of another popular form, that of the detective story—perhaps the 19th-century's most vivid expression of the necessary "second reading" implicit in all narrative. Speaking of this apparently demotic genre and its paradigmatic usefulness in understanding fictional plots, Tzvetan Todorov describes the temporal structure of the classic "whodunit" as a deliberate—indeed unavoidable—conflation of two stories, the "absent" story of the crime and the belated story of the inquisition: in solving the crime the detective does not merely identify the culprit or the criminal, he also postulates a sequence of events leading up to the crime which is, and can only be, a later retracing of an earlier occurrence. In this way, Todorov suggests, the "paradoxical" structure of detective fiction might serve to elucidate the representational strategy of all narrative discourse, in particular its inevitable fusion of *fabula* (or story) and *sju̇žet* (or plot) as a way of organizing its fictional material.

In the undeniable sense that *Benito Cereno*'s plot consists of an elaborate series of retellings or retracings—Delano's bumbling attempt to interpret (and then reinterpret) the "enigmatic" events aboard the *San Dominick,* Don Benito's authorized or official version of the mutiny embodied in the deposition, even the reader's "retrospective" judgment of the story based on these two accounts—one might easily infer that the fundamental form of the work is that of a detective story *manqué:* not only is there a crime (and so presumably a criminal), there is also a series of "investigators" at work intent on discovering "what really happened" aboard the *San Dominick* before Don Benito's desperate leap into Delano's boat. Reinforcing this notion of narrative belatedness or secondariness in *Benito Cereno* is the compositional history of the work itself. As Harold H. Scudder noted, Melville derived his 1855 narrative in part from an 1817 naval document written by the "real" Amasa Delano, a document historically recounting, among other things, a violent slave-revolt on the high seas. In his fictionalization of this event (as well as of the *Amistad* mutiny and the *Creole* affair described by Kaplan) Melville thus undertakes a task of detection or reconstruction even more arduous than that assigned to Todorov's detective. As author, he must construct a version of the crime that is not once but twice removed from its mortal matrix, whereby his version is constrained to be nothing more than a later retelling of an earlier text.

As a detective story, therefore, *Benito Cereno* clearly anticipates the belated structures and "absent" centers of such essentially modernist works as James's "The Figure in the Carpet," Conrad's *Heart of Darkness,* or even Faulkner's *Absalom, Absalom!,* whose ostensive aim is the detailed recollection and retelling of an earlier story or event from a later point of view. Like these other narratives of deferred transmission, Melville's text reveals a persistent slippage between the earlier or absent story (in this case, Babo's original take-over of the ship) and its putative retelling in the narrative, a slippage which is formally elaborated in the relation between Delano's story and the legal deposition which follows it. Insofar as Delano's perception of events in the first half of the narrative invites comparison to the reading of a text, we are thus reminded of our initial reading of *Benito Cereno*—a reading shaped to a significant degree by Melville's "immoderate" use of stereotypical plotting ("the *other* way" of writing) in the creation of his story. Judging from most recent reactions, however,

Delano's reading or misreading of events aboard the *San Dominick* is one we have come to regard with considerable antagonism and contempt.

—John Haegert, "Voicing Slavery through Silence: Narrative Mutiny in Melville's *Benito Cereno*," *Mosaic* 26, No. 2 (Spring 1993): 27–28

Books by
Herman Melville

Typee: A Peep at Polynesian Life. 1846. 2 vols.

Omoo: A Narrative of Adventures in the South Seas. 1847.

Mardi: And a Voyage Thither. 1849. 2 vols.

Redburn: His First Voyage: Being the Sailor-Boy Confessions and Reminiscences of the Son-of-a-Gentleman, in the Merchant Service. 1849.

White-Jacket; or, The World in a Man-of-War. 1850.

Moby-Dick; or, The Whale. 1851.

Pierre; or, The Ambiguities. 1852.

Israel Potter: His Fifty Years of Exile. 1855.

The Piazza Tales. 1856.

The Confidence-Man: His Masquerade. 1857.

Battle-Pieces and Aspects of the War. 1866.

Clarel: A Poem and Pilgrimage in the Holy Land. 1876. 2 vols.

John Marr and Other Sailors with Some Sea-Pieces. 1888.

Timoleon, etc. 1891.

Some Personal Letters and a Bibliography. Ed. Meade Minnigerode. 1922.

Works (Standard Edition). 1922–24. 16 vols.

The Apple-Tree and Other Sketches. Ed. Henry Chapin. 1922.

Journal Up the Straits: October 11, 1856–May 5, 1857. Ed. Raymond Weaver. 1935.

Collected Poems. Ed. Howard P. Vincent. 1947.

Complete Stories. Ed. Jay Leyda. 1949.

Journal of a Visit to London and the Continent 1849–1850.
Ed. Eleanor Melville Metcalf. 1948.

The Portable Melville. Ed. Jay Leyda. 1952.

Letters. Ed. Merrell R. Davis and William H. Gilman. 1960.

Writings (Northwestern-Newberry Edition). Ed. Harrison
Hayford et al. 1968–93. 15 vols. (to date).

At the Hostelry and Naples in the Time of Bomba.
Ed. Gordon Poole. 1989.

Works about Herman Melville and *Billy Budd,* "Benito Cereno," and "Bartleby the Scrivener"

Berthoff, Werner. *The Example of Melville.* Princeton: Princeton University Press, 1962.

Bewley, Marius. "Melville." In Bewley's *The Eccentric Design: Form in the Classic American Novel.* New York: Columbia University Press, 1959, pp. 187–219.

Bickley, R. Bruce, Jr. *The Method of Melville's Short Fiction 1853–1856.* Durham, NC: Duke University Press, 1975.

Blackmur, R. P. "The Craft of Herman Melville: A Putative Statement." In Blackmur's *The Lion and the Honeycomb: Essays in Solicitude and Critique.* New York: Harcourt, Brace & World, 1955, pp. 124–44.

Bloom, Harold, ed. *Herman Melville's* Billy Budd, Benito Cereno, Bartleby the Scrivener, *and Other Tales.* New York: Chelsea House, 1987.

Bowen, Merlin. *The Long Encounter: Self and Experience in the Writings of Herman Melville.* Chicago: University of Chicago Press, 1960.

Brodhead, Richard H. *Hawthorne, Melville, and the Novel.* Chicago: University of Chicago Press, 1976.

Brooks, Van Wyck. *The Times of Melville and Whitman.* New York: Dutton, 1947.

Bryant, John. *Melville and Repose: The Rhetoric of Humor in the American Renaissance.* New York: Oxford University Press, 1993.

Cameron, Sharon. *The Corporeal Self: Allegories of the Body in Melville and Hawthorne.* Baltimore: Johns Hopkins University Press, 1981.

Canaday, Nicholas, Jr. *Melville and Authority.* Gainesville: University of Florida Press, 1968.

Cardozo Studies in Law and Literature 1, No. 1 (Spring 1989). Special *Billy Budd* issue.

Coale, Samuel Chase. *In Hawthorne's Shadow: American Romance from Melville to Mailer.* Lexington: University Press of Kentucky, 1985.

Dillingham, William B. *Melville's Short Fiction 1853–1856.* Athens: University of Georgia Press, 1977.

Dimock, Wai-Chee. *Empire for Liberty: Melville and the Poets of Individualism.* Princeton: Princeton University Press, 1988.

Douglas, Ann. "Herman Melville and the Revolt against the Reader." In Douglas's *The Feminization of American Culture.* New York: Knopf, 1978, pp. 289–326.

Dryden, Edgar A. *Melville's Thematics of Form: The Great Art of Telling the Truth.* Baltimore: Johns Hopkins University Press, 1968.

Finkelstein, Dorothee Metlitsky. *Melville's Orienda.* New Haven: Yale University Press, 1961.

Fisher, Marvin. *Going Under: Melville's Short Fiction and the American 1850s.* Baton Rouge: Louisiana State University Press, 1977.

Fogle, Richard Harter. *Melville's Shorter Tales.* Norman: University of Oklahoma Press, 1960.

Franklin, H. Bruce. *The Wake of the Gods: Melville's Mythology.* Stanford: Stanford University Press, 1963.

Fredericks, Nancy. *Melville's Art of Democracy.* Athens: University of Georgia Press, 1995.

Garner, Stanton. *The Civil War World of Herman Melville.* Lawrence: University Press of Kansas, 1993.

Grenberg, Bruce I. *Some Other World to Find: Quest and Negation in the Works of Herman Melville.* Urbana: University of Illinois Press, 1989.

Haberstroh, Charles J., Jr. *Melville and Male Identity.* Rutherford, NJ: Fairleigh Dickinson University Press, 1980.

Horsley-Meachem, Gloria. "Bull of the Nile: Symbol, History, and Racial Myth in 'Benito Cereno.'" *New England Quarterly* 64 (1991): 225–42.

Humphreys, A. R. *Melville.* Edinburgh: Oliver & Boyd, 1962.

Inge, M. Thomas, ed. *Bartleby the Inscrutable: A Collection of Commentary on Herman Melville's Tale "Bartleby the Scrivener."* Hamden, CT: Shoe String Press, 1979.

Karcher, Carolyn L. *Shadow over the Promised Land: Slavery, Race, and Violence in Melville's America.* Baton Rouge: Louisiana State University Press, 1980.

Lee, A. Robert, ed. *Herman Melville: Reassessments.* London: Vision Press; Totowa, NJ: Barnes & Noble, 1984.

Levin, Harry. *The Power of Blackness: Hawthorne, Poe, and Melville.* New York: Knopf, 1958.

Levine, Robert S. "Follow Your Leader: Captains and Mutineers in Herman Melville's *Benito Cereno.*" In Levine's *Conspiracy and Romance: Studies in Brockden Brown, Cooper, Hawthorne, and Melville.* New York: Cambridge University Press, 1989, pp. 165–230.

Leyda, Jay. *The Melville Log: A Documentary Life of Herman Melville 1819–1891.* New York: Harcourt, Brace, 1951. 2 vols.

McCall, Dan. *The Silence of Bartleby.* Ithaca, NY: Cornell University Press, 1989.

McCarthy, Paul. *"The Twisted Mind": Madness in Melville's Fiction.* Iowa City: University of Iowa Press, 1990.

McWilliams, John P., Jr. *Hawthorne, Melville, and the American Character: A Looking-Glass Business.* Cambridge: Cambridge University Press, 1984.

Miller, Edwin Haviland. *Melville.* New York: George Braziller, 1975.

Miller, Perry. *The Raven and the Whale: The War of Words and Wits in the Era of Poe and Melville.* New York: Harcourt, Brace, 1956.

Moore, Richard S. *That Cunning Alphabet: Melville's Aesthetics of Nature.* Amsterdam: Rodopi, 1982.

Mumford, Lewis. *Herman Melville.* New York: Harcourt, Brace, 1929.

Nnolim, Charles E. *Melville's "Benito Cereno": A Study in the Meaning of Name Symbolism.* New York: New Voices, 1974.

Parker, Hershel. *Reading* Billy Budd. Evanston, IL: Northwestern University Press, 1990.

Pommer, Henry. *Milton and Melville.* Pittsburgh: University of Pittsburgh Press, 1950.

Pops, Martin Leonard. *The Melville Archetype.* Kent, OH: Kent State University Press, 1970.

Reynolds, David S. *Beneath the American Renaissance: The Subversive Imagination in the Age of Emerson and Melville.* New York: Knopf, 1988.

Rogin, Michael Paul. *Subversive Genealogy: The Politics and Art of Herman Melville.* New York: Knopf, 1983.

Schirmeister, Pamela. *The Consolations of Space: The Place of Romance in Hawthorne, Melville, and James.* Stanford: Stanford University Press, 1990.

Short, Bryan Collier. *Cast by Means of Figures: Herman Melville's Rhetorical Development.* Amherst: University of Massachusetts Press, 1992.

Simpson, David. *Fetishism and Imagination: Dickens, Melville, Conrad.* Baltimore: Johns Hopkins University Press, 1982.

Suchoff, David. *Critical Theory and the Novel: Mass Society and Cultural Criticism in Dickens, Melville, and Kafka.* Madison: University of Wisconsin Press, 1994.

Sundquist, Eric J. " 'Benito Cereno' and New World Slavery." In *Reconstructing American Literary History,* ed. Sacvan Bercovitch. Cambridge, MA: Harvard University Press, 1986, pp. 93–122.

Thompson, Lawrance. *Melville's Quarrel with God.* Princeton: Princeton University Press, 1952.

Tolchin, Neal L. *Mourning, Gender, and Creativity in the Art of Herman Melville.* New Haven: Yale University Press, 1988.

Widmer, Kingsley. *The Ways of Nihilism: A Study of Herman Melville's Short Novels.* Los Angeles: California State Colleges, 1970.

Winters, Yvor. "Herman Melville and the Problem of Moral Navigation." In Winters's *In Defense of Reason.* New York: Swallow Press/William Morrow, 1947, pp. 200–233.

Young, Philip. *The Private Melville.* University Park: Pennsylvania State University Press, 1993.

Index of
Themes and Ideas